CELEBRATING
CHILDREN'S
BOOKS

CELEBRATING CHILDREN'S BOOKS

Essays
on Children's Literature
in Honor of
Zena Sutherland

Edited by Betsy Hearne and Marilyn Kaye

Lothrop, Lee & Shepard Books
New York

Library of Congress Cataloging in Publication Data
Main entry under title:
Celebrating children's books.
1. Children's literature—History and criticism—Addresses, essays,
lectures. 2. Sutherland, Zena—Addresses, essays, lectures.
I. Sutherland, Zena. II. Hearne, Betsy Gould. III. Kaye, Marilyn.
PN1009.A1C38   809'89282   81–2626
ISBN 0–688–00752–X AACR2

Printed in the United States of America.
First Edition
1 2 3 4 5 6 7 8 9 10

Acknowledgments

From "Tree and Leaf" by J.R.R. Tolkien, in Betsy Hearne's "Innocence & Experience: A Critical Paradox." Copyright © 1964 by George Allen & Unwin Ltd. Reprinted by permission of Houghton Mifflin Company and George Allen & Unwin Publishers Ltd.

For excerpts in Myra Cohn Livingston's "Nonsense Verse: The Complete Escape" we gratefully acknowledge the following:

"Poundcake from Ealing" from *Hurry, Hurry, Mary Dear! and Other Nonsense Poems* by N.M. Bodecker. Copyright © 1976 by N.M. Bodecker. Used with the permission of Margaret K. McElderry Books/Atheneum Publishers and J. M. Dent & Sons Ltd.

From *Opposites* by Richard Wilbur, copyright © 1973 by Richard Wilbur. Reprinted by permission of Harcourt Brace Jovanovich Inc.

"Pome" from *One at a Time* by David McCord has been reprinted by permission of Little, Brown and Company.

"Flonster Poem" from *The Snopp on the Sidewalk and Other Poems* by Jack Prelutsky. Text copyright © 1976, 1977 by Jack Prelutsky. Reprinted by permission of Greenwillow Books (A Division of William Morrow & Company).

"Exploding Gravy" from *One Winter Night in August and Other Nonsense Rhymes* by X.J. Kennedy. Copyright © 1975 by X.J. Kennedy. Used with

CONTENTS

A Tribute to
Zena Sutherland

꘎

Sophie Silberberg

This volume of essays devoted to the art of writing and publishing books for children is a celebration in honor of Zena Sutherland, one of America's most respected reviewers of books for children, an admired teacher of children's literature, a prominent anthologist, and a leader of considerable influence within the many professions concerned with children and their reading. Since 1958, when she became Editor of the *Bulletin of the Center for Children's Books* of the University of Chicago, Mrs. Sutherland's career has paralleled one of the most interesting and prolific periods in children's book publishing. This lively period has been marked by significant sociological, cultural, and attitudinal changes—changes that seem to be mirrored instantaneously in the books published for children and young adults.

Gathered together here are essays exploring various aspects of the craft of writing, illustrating, and publishing for children and young adults, by an outstanding group of individuals who have achieved success in the field. What these essayists have in common is their mutual respect and admiration for Mrs. Sutherland as a critic and a friend. Each contributor has selected an aspect of his or her own work to write about. As a whole, *Celebrating Children's Books* becomes a valuable resource for both the creators and users of children's books—for teachers, librarians, and youth workers; for writers, illustrators, and all concerned with the publishing and distribution of books for children.

Of the personal and professional qualities that led Mrs. Sutherland to become a guiding force in this period in the history of children's literature, foremost is her deep respect for children and their reading tastes. This respect encompasses her deep conviction that, given the opportunity, children want to learn, to grapple with ideas and understand issues of our day as well as those of history. Of equal importance to her art as a critic is the openness of spirit with which she has approached and reacted to the changing mores and nontraditional ideas that were upsetting to many and forced a rethinking and redefinition of our perception of long-held values. This spirit helped Mrs. Sutherland to emerge as a balancing force between those rushing change for change's sake and those who would resist any change. Then there is Zena Sutherland, the warm and trusted friend of authors, illustrators, editors, publishers' representatives, librarians, teaching colleagues, and devoted students. To her credit, the strong bonds of these friendships have never interfered with her objectivity as a book critic but rather have served to strengthen her capacity to inspire, to support, and to challenge.

As a reviewer, Zena Sutherland can always be counted on to delve into the very heart of the book before her and to articulate her opinions about it in a straightforward and lucid style. The accessibility of her reviews has nurtured the publication and readership of works of literary and artistic merit, as well as supported a wide range of important, useful works of fiction and nonfiction. Without being an active crusader for bibliotherapy, as such, Zena can always be depended on to identify those situations and ideas that respond to the concerns of children and help place these concerns in their proper context.

Celebrating Children's Books has been a labor of love for the contributors, the advisory committee, and the publisher. The royalties derived from the sale and distribution of this publication will be contributed to the establishment of the Zena Sutherland Lectureship Fund at the University of Chicago, the base of her many-faceted career.

Chicago, Illinois, is home for Zena. She earned both her undergraduate degree and master's in library science at the University. In 1972 she added to her responsibilities as Editor of the prestigious *Bulletin* by joining the staff of the Graduate Library School of the University of Chicago as a lecturer. In 1977 she became an associate professor in this department. While her reviewing skills have guided librarians and teachers, she has also reached out to a larger circle of book audiences. From 1972 to 1977 she was the widely read contributing editor for children's books at the *Saturday Review*. In 1977 she joined the staff of the *Chicago Tribune* as the children's book review editor.

When Mrs. Sutherland succeeded the famed May Hill Arbuthnot as the author of *Children and Books*, the volume that forms the basis of so many children's literature courses, she became the mentor of teachers and librarians who work to bring books and children together. Mrs. Sutherland is also the editor of *The Best in Children's Books*, a compilation of recommended reviews that have appeared in the *Bulletin.* She is always in demand as a speaker at meetings devoted to literature for children and is a frequent contributor of reviews and opinions on wide ranges of professional and nonprofessional publications and journals, among them the *World Book,* the *Compton Yearbook, Library Quarterly,* and *Library Trends.*

Mrs. Sutherland has served as a member of all of the most important prestigious award committees honoring books for children. She was appointed to the very first committee established for a National Book Award in the children's book category in 1969. She has been a member of several American Library Association Newbery-Caldecott Award committees and she chaired the 1975 committee.

Her perceptive talents enriched the international field when she served on the Hans Christian Andersen Award Jury for two consecutive two-year terms. Among the other award committees that have benefited from her participation and leadership are the Mildred Batchelder Award, the Jane Addams Award, and the recently established International Reading Association Book Award.

In the words of John Rowe Townsend: "At present good reviewers of children's books are probably scarcer than good writers of them. And it is almost as necessary that there should be good and effective writing about children's books as that there should be good children's books. . . . Not the least important thing about good reviewing is that it's good for authors, who need to be encouraged, stimulated, disciplined, needled, and challenged into doing their best. . . . Only the best will do." And *the best* is what Zena Sutherland is.

CREATING
THE
BOOKS

The Grammar
of Story

∾

Lloyd Alexander

By inventing language, the human race invented story. Words can state a fact: "The straw was yellow." Or work magic: "The straw was spun into gold." Story need not be verbal. Pictures can tell a story. Music plays out wordless dramas, different at every hearing. We can dance a story. But my interest here is with story in the form of language, its underlying mechanisms and structures: the grammar of story.

In story, the dividing line is not necessarily between fact and fiction. The line, that is, can be stretched very thin. Some fiction claims to be true. We call it history. Some truth claims to be fiction. We call it literature. Both are aspects of story, nonetheless. In the broad sense of the word, story ranges from the Book of Job to the report of a street accident. Once we go beyond the simplest declaration of fact to give an account with any degree of complexity, we are obliged to select, arrange, emphasize—to become storytellers.

In *War and Peace,* for example, during his first battle

young Nikolai Rostov falls off his horse, badly hurts his arm, and runs panic-stricken from a French hussar. Later, safe with his comrades, he intends to tell everything exactly as it happened. Instead, he gets carried away by his report. Like every soldier, he describes the battle as he wishes it had been, and himself as gloriously heroic.

"If he had told the truth to his listeners, they would not have believed him," writes Tolstoy. "They expected to hear how he had swept down like a tempest, how his saber had tasted blood and he had fallen exhausted. And these are the things he told them."

The passage bites deeper because Tolstoy has previously given us a scene describing "everything exactly as it happened." But even Tolstoy cannot encompass "everything." His genius is making it seem that way.

Storytellers, in realism or fantasy, create illusions, not clinical studies. The test of the latter is how accurately they convey specific facts. The test of illusion is how thoroughly it convinces us of its reality; how strongly it resonates in our emotions; how deeply it moves us to new feelings and new insights. Such illusions may be the truest things we know. "Art," says Picasso, "is a lie that lets us see the truth."

As a conscious work of art, story tries—as all art does —to make sense of a world not especially noted for making much sense at all. To help it do this, to help in its creation, a fairly small number of elements are available. As grammar sets language in order, these elements help to structure illusion. They are seldom used singly. Part of a story's richness lies in combining them in varying degrees.

In the grammar of story, we might call the "subject" the people we choose to tell about. But these should not be static figures. Adjectives describing them are not enough. If character is to be revealed, developed, or tested, the subject must take action.

As the verb provides the driving energy of a sentence, the "verb" of story is conflict, classically of three types: conflict with nature (*Robinson Crusoe,* for example); conflict with other people (the epic battles of *The Iliad* and the domestic tensions of, say, *Little Women*); conflict with oneself— the arena of the heart, crowded with opposing desires and ambivalences (the inner turmoil of *Crime and Punishment*).

The "direct object" is the point toward which character and conflict lead us. But we need to know what the characters are striving to do, what helps or hinders them, how they succeed or fail. In other words, plot.

A well-crafted plot, like some remarkable clockwork, can fascinate us by its sheer ingenuity. Or we may not even be aware of the plot, the happenings appearing simply to grow as imperceptibly as a tree. Out of context, a given plot may seem utterly ridiculous.

Many of the great nineteenth-century novels have plots so outrageously implausible that a freshman in a creative writing class would be flunked out for suggesting anything like them. Dickens was one of the worst offenders. Genius though he was, he reveled in cases of mistaken identity, farfetched coincidences, look-alikes, hidden documents. In *Bleak House,* one of the plot points involves a character bursting into flames by spontaneous combustion. Even Dickens must have been uneasy about that one, since he felt obliged to defend it, in his preface, with supposedly scientific data. (Nevertheless, despite the spontaneous combustion, *Bleak House* remains a masterpiece.)

Today, we like to think our plots are much more sensible. Future readers, however, may find them as quaint as the costumes of an earlier age. Fashions change, in literature as well as Levis. Much as we admire them, our ancestors often strike us as just a touch naive. I have no reason to believe we shall escape that same judgment.

This is only to point out a paradox—and story is filled with paradox. While the bones and joints of plot must be strong enough to support the living body of story, in the long run I believe plot is one of the least important elements. Plot is not the same as story.

Plot, say, is the road on which we drive our car. The road may have unforeseen turns, alarming bumps, and potholes; it may plunge downhill and delightfully scare the wits out of us. But if plot is the road, story is what we see along the way.

There, I think, lies the real interest. If we ask someone, especially a young person, to tell us what a story is about, they are likely to start at the beginning and go through all the episodes to the end, externals being always easier to describe. But what we keep for ourselves, what we remember best, sometimes all our lives, are individual moments: "I liked the part where . . ." or "It was great when . . ." Such moments move us deeply without our being especially aware of what brought us to them in the first place.

This is not to minimize the pleasure we derive from an elegant plot, by which we can hardly help but be intrigued. The French word for "plot" is, appropriately, *l'intrigue.* But why, indeed, are we intrigued? One reason might be that plot evokes the eternal and eternally vexing question of free will and determinism.

According to Jung, if we thoroughly investigate the antecedents of an event, we will find no such thing as coincidence. The concept of karma, the inexorable working out of the effects of our deeds, has been a persuasive idea in Eastern culture. And yet, our life experiences convince us that there are, in fact, coincidences, strokes of luck, random happenings.

Plot allows us to have it both ways; to accept both notions simultaneously. In one aspect, plot is an exercise in causality. Or a demonstration of the inevitable. Our pleasure comes both from realizing a plot had to work out as it did and being surprised at discovering how. In another aspect, plot gives the impression of a series of free choices, of decisions deliberately taken. Conflict, the dynamic element of story, sooner or later must come to the moment of choice, not merely instinctive reaction (though I suppose we could say we "choose" to duck if somebody throws a rock at us). We may see plot as a sequence of conscious decisions— sometimes right, sometimes wrong, careful or hasty, but conscious, nevertheless.

Characters, conflict, and the working out of conflict give us the equivalent of a simple sentence. Everything else feeds into and reinforces it. Adjectives, adverbs, dependent and independent clauses correspond to other devices and principles.

An example would be what Alfred Hitchcock calls "The McGuffin," a marvelous term for the basic premise of a story. It may be an idea, a situation, or some physical object. The premise may be quite simple, the simpler the better. But, generally, what gives the premise its initial energy and helps to generate continuing energy is a small but important turn of the idea: something like the one twist that changes a paper ribbon from a loop into a Möbius strip. Two young people are desperately in love—but their families hate each other. An elderly man reads tales of noble chivalry—but takes them as literal guides to everyday behavior. (There's a hidden joker in all this. Every one of us can invent premises by the dozen. The trick is in what we do with them. As in music, in sonata form, it's not only the statement of theme but the development that really counts.)

Suspense has always been one of the great elements of story: on the level of simple curiosity ("What happens next?") to unbearably delicious agony ("The suspense is killing me!") The more we know, and the less the characters know, about a situation, the greater the suspense. To paraphrase Alfred Hitchcock, if someone explodes a bomb in the living room the result is shock. But if we know someone has hidden a time bomb in a closet, while the characters, in blissful ignorance, enjoy themselves at a party, the result is suspense.

As for economy, the writer does well to play the role of a skinflint boss, never hiring new personnel when it is possible to get extra work from the existing staff. Characters, incidents, and objects may be interesting in themselves, but if they do not pull their own weight, if they contribute nothing to the overall pattern, the storyteller had best dismiss them. Otherwise, both writer and reader may be embarrassed by unemployed characters standing around shuffling their feet. Or, as Chekhov puts it, if we are shown a loaded pistol in the first act, somebody must pull the trigger before the last act.

Creation, in its early stages and, to one degree or another, during all others, is a nonrational process. Nonrational, however, is not irrational. After the first creative spark, the logic of imagination should be as rigorous as Euclid's. Storytellers have the privilege of inventing their own logic. They depart from it at their peril. What helps to make the logic of story logical is preparation. Within the frame of their story, playing by their own rules, storytellers can cause almost anything to happen by preparing for it in advance, by laying the groundwork for future actions. If we want to hoist the enginer, we must first build the petar. Early establishment of character traits and potential turns of events make them organic to the story. Otherwise, they are gratuitous. Incidents in real life may depend on the gratuitous act, but story is not real life.

If the "direct object" of story is plot, the "indirect object" is the subtext of the work. What the story is about is not always what the story is about. *Don Quixote,* ultimately, is not about a harmless eccentric who mistakes windmills for giants. Or, as Woody Allen commented after speed-reading *War and Peace:* "It's about Russia."

Storytellers may not be aware of their subtexts, nor do they need to be. They may understand them only later, if ever. Subtext has more to do with attitude than intellect. It is not tacked on—we don't dig the foundation after the house is built. It comes from the bone marrow of the storyteller. It includes tonality, flavor, a personal way of looking at the world—all intangible, all very real. As a poet described it: "A taste in the head."

And here, at this point, grammar offers little help. We can learn all the foregoing, in greater detail better expressed, from any book on narrative technique. We can follow all the rules and precepts earnestly and diligently and never breathe life into a story. On the other hand, I can easily imagine a storyteller happily ignoring all conventional wisdom, shattering rules left and right, and creating masterpieces.

"Art begins where technique ends," says Leopold Auer, the great violin teacher. A despairing fiddler, I know to my dismay how true it is. We can do it all right and have it come out all wrong. This applies to every art. Having done something once or a thousand times does not guarantee our doing it well or even doing it again. In art, there are no guarantees. Creation, whatever its form, is not an act of will, but an act of faith.

Grammar, in the long run, offers only tantalizing clues to the nature and function of story. It does not define them. I am not at all sure they can be defined, given the limitations of language and the limitations of our present knowledge. Score analysis shows how Mozart's G-Minor Quintet works; why it works remains a mystery.

The same holds true for story. However, if we hope to come anywhere close to understanding its essence, I think we must try to discover how it relates, on deepest levels, to social and psychological history (if, indeed, there is much difference between the two).

Linguists have speculated on the existence of deep structures common to all languages. Cultural anthropologists have done likewise in studying mythologies. So far, they have no definitive answers. I would be out of my competence to offer anything definitive about the nature of story. The best I can do is restate the obvious, and suggest the underlying unity of story and other human activities.

The raw materials of story are the raw materials of all human cultures. Story deals with the same questions as theology, philosophy, psychology. It is concerned with polarities: love and hate, birth and death, joy and sorrow, loss and recovery.

But I would also suggest that story evokes and reflects other conditions. Though Joseph Campbell, among others, offers the basic hero-tale as the central myth of human culture, I think we might add some other ingredients that make story so attractive to us.

Earlier I mentioned plot as demonstrating the inevitable and at the same time giving the impression of free choice. We believe we do make free choices. Yet we often feel we are bit players in some incomprehensible scenario that we had no hand in writing. Story, perhaps, reconciles us and helps us to accept this terrifying contradiction—to live with it and still keep our sanity. Perhaps this accounts for the sense of satisfaction, I would even say "consolation," we feel when a story has ended rightly: not a question of happy or unhappy ending, but the rightness of it.

Story, I think, also tells us very simply that actions have consequences; that we can learn to deal with surprise and reversal, and are capable of making decisions; that we may hope in the face of hopelessness—and survive.

We might speculate that the emotions and states of mind we experience in story even have some correspondence with children's games. Children play hopscotch on an ancient pattern symbolizing death and rebirth. Is it too far-fetched to see in a game of tag some reflection of the hand of fate singling us out as "It"? Hide-and-seek, king of the hill, ringolevio—to what extent do they reflect the skills and emotions involved in hunting and fighting, capturing and rescuing prisoners? To what extent do they give models of courage, cowardice, loyalty, betrayal? In one guise or another, these are some basic story models. (There is, regrettably, little research available on female games and initiation mysteries. Between them and their male counterparts, I suspect we should find more similarities than differences.)

However closely they reflect social and psychological history, stories, like games, take place in a suspended moment of time. Even the most realistic and topical story is not happening *now,* although it pretends to be. All stories happen *in illo tempore,* as Mircea Eliade calls it: in primordial "Great Time," which is the time of art, not history. Films and television, modern media and ancient story, make us live, states Eliade, "in time of a quality quite other than that of secular duration . . . which evokes a profound echo in the spectator."

We need not rely on metaphysics or aesthetics to give us a clue to the nature of story. It may be inside our heads. Carl Sagan, in *The Dragons of Eden,* lists several common categories of dreams: falling; being pursued or attacked; attempting repeatedly and unsuccessfully to perform a task; having diverse sexual experiences. These, too, figure among the materials of story. While fear of falling seems clearly connected with our arboreal origins, the other categories, according to Sagan, "correspond to aggressive, hierarchical, ritualistic, and sexual functions." This, he points out, is the realm of the brain's R-Complex: the most ancient part of the neural chassis, which we share with the other mammals and even with the reptiles.

Perhaps, then, story is born not from language but anatomy. The grammar of story may be the grammar of the human brain.

If there is, in fact, a grammar of story, the language it shapes is a *lingua franca,* a common language for all of us. Story, finally, is humanity's autobiography.

Escaping into Ourselves

∽

Susan Cooper

The legs turn toward the library, the hands reach for a novel. Why? "Well, I read for pleasure, of course." Of course: but what's the root of the pleasure, the reason why anyone, child or adult, reads fiction?

The reason, simply, is entertainment. The novel entertains by offering refreshment, solace, excitement, relaxation, perhaps even inspiration: an escape from reality. And the escape, in turn, brings encouragement, leaving the reader fortified to cope with his own reality when he returns to it. So I hear the slam of the door sometimes as my twelve-year-old Kate, feeling the weight of the world upon her slender shoulders, retreats into her room; and I know that she will shortly be curled up in there with a book—and will, afterward, feel better.

In "realistic" fiction, the escape and the encouragement come from a sense of parallel: from finding a true and recognizable portrait of real life. In those pages we encounter familiar problems, but they're *someone else's* problems; involved but secure, relaxing into the story, we watch while the other fellow copes. If the ending is happy, we are reassured; even in a difficult world, all may be well at last. If the ending is tragic, the ancient cathartic effect of pity and fear takes over and we are reassured just the same, by the courage or steadfastness or simple humanity of the hero/heroine. We small people enjoy reading—need to read—about big people; at one end of that scale is the newspaper gossip column, at the other the New Testament.

Comic novels, thrillers, biographies, romances all have the same kind of appeal. So does science fiction, which does unearthly things to space and time but is still realistic fiction at heart. In all such books the reader knows, beneath the suspense of the story, what to expect; the "straight" novelist will not tamper with the limits of human behavior, nor the science fiction writer cheat by changing the laws of thermodynamics. Their greatest charm is that they play an exciting game according to rules.

There is just one kind of fiction which differs from all these. Why does anyone read, or write, fantasy?

Fantasy goes one stage beyond realism; requiring complete intellectual surrender, it asks more of the reader, and at its best may offer more. Perhaps this is why it is also less popular, at any rate among adults, who set such store by their ability to think. Among small children, who have not yet begun to think much about the stories they hear, fantasy reigns supreme. No realistic story has yet attained the universal affection they give to fairy-tale, except possibly, in the United States, *Goodnight Moon*—which is not a story at all, but a deceptively simple ritual. Very young children, their conscious minds not yet developed, are all feeling and instinct. Closer to the unconscious than they will ever be again, they respond naturally to the archetypes and the deep echoes of fairy story, ritual, and myth.

But after that, learning begins, as it must; the child is launched on his long quest for understanding. As he discovers the world around him, and the books which show him that world, his tastes in reading veer naturally toward realism. Some children not only reach that point but stay there; shunning fantasy as "babyish," they grow up to become those adults who seldom read novels at all, and find their escape and encouragement from those other contemporary escapist phenomena, which range, as Ursula Le Guin once wryly observed, from television soap operas to "that masterpiece of total unreality, the daily Stock Market Report." But others, born with a different chemistry, go on seeking out fantasy all their lives, instinctively aware that so far from being babyish, it is probably the most complex form of fiction they will ever find.

And what do we, and they, find, when we read fantasy? The escape and encouragement are there, for sure—but in a different form. This time, when we depart from our own reality into the reality of the book, it's not a matter of stepping across the street, or into the next county, or even the next planet. This time, we're going out of time, out of space, into the unconscious, that dreamlike world which has in it all the images and emotions accumulated since the human race began. We aren't escaping out, we're escaping in, without any idea of what we may encounter. Fantasy is the metaphor through which we discover ourselves.

So it is for the writer, too. Every book is a voyage of discovery. Perhaps I speak only for myself, perhaps it's different for other writers; but for me, the making of a fantasy is quite unlike the relatively ordered procedure of writing any other kind of book. I've never actually *thought:* "I am writing fantasy"; one simply sits down to write whatever book is knocking to be let out. But in hindsight, I can see the peculiar difference in approach. When working on a book which turns out to be a fantasy novel, I exist in a state of continual astonishment. The work begins with a deep breath and a blindly trusting step into the unknown; I know where I'm going, and who's going with me, but I have no real idea of what I shall find on the way, or whom I'll meet. Each time, I am striking out into a strange land, listening for the music that will tell me which way to go. And I am always overcome by wonder, and a kind of unfocused gratitude, when I arrive; and I always think of Eliot:

> We shall not cease from exploration
> And the end of all our exploring
> Will be to arrive where we started
> And know the place for the first time. . . .

One of our best "realistic" novelists (how I hate these labels—but there's no way round them) said to me once, cheerfully rude, "Oh, you fantasy people have it so easy, you don't know you're born. If there's a problem in your plot—bingo, you bring in a bit of magic, and the problem's gone."

No, no, no, fantasy doesn't work that way; anyone cherishing such theories is bound for trouble. If he or she tries to sail our perilous sea in such a ship, he is likely to end up with a book which may be is beautifully written, hugely entertaining, full of bits of magic—but which somehow isn't fantasy. True fantasy is John Masefield's *The Box of Delights,* or Alan Garner's *The Owl Service:* books which cast a spell so subtle and overwhelming that it has overpowered the reader's imagination, carried him outside all rules, before he has noticed what is happening. To some degree I doubt whether Masefield or Garner or the rest knew what was happening either; they simply heard the music, and employed all their very considerable talent to write it down. You can't write fantasy on purpose. It won't come when called. Like poetry, it is a kind of happy accident which overtakes certain writers before they are born.

In case I seem to be portraying those of us who write fantasy as The Chosen, I might add that all other specific gifts within the large realm of fiction are just as slippery, just as arbitrary. Very few writers can sow their seed successfully in more than one or two fields. Once, when I was young and very poor, I decided to chase an instant income by writing short stories for women's magazines. This wasn't my favorite occupation, but I knew I could write, and— believing that therefore I could write absolutely anything— I did my best. The stories were uniformly terrible and not one of them was published. Wiser and less arrogant—and still poor—I went back to the kind of writing I was born to do: that is, to the limited range of ideas that my imagination would offer unbidden. And those writers with a different kind of imagination, hearing a different music, went on writing very good short stories.

An entry in one of my working notebooks reads: "We are all at the mercy of the quality of the imagination we inherit. The book can never be better than that."

A writer's notebooks are perhaps the best illustration (better in some ways than the books themselves) of the way his mind works. Some consist of detailed blueprints for books or plays, set out with mathematical precision; some are filled with discursive examinations of character, building up backgrounds which may never appear in the story but which show the writer getting to know the people he has made. My own notes are mostly cryptic and random, full of images, scattered with quotations and ideas which often seem totally irrelevant to the book in hand—though they weren't at the time. Rereading them, I have always again the *feel* of what it is like to write fantasy, though whether any of this can be communicated by the notes themselves I do not know.

> This book is mountains and lakes and valleys, birds and trees, with the sea in the distance glimmering, waiting. The last book is the lost cantref off the estuary, the drowned land where the bells sound. The long sands, the open sea and sky; the dunes.

∽

> If you wear agrimony, you may see witches. And if you look into their eyes, you see no reflection of yourself. The scarlet pimpernel is a charm against them.

∽

> Names of fields in Hitcham: Great and Lower Cogmarthon; Upper and Lower Brissels; Homer Corner; Hogg Hill.

∽

The sword comes from the drowned land.

∽

The opening of doors. Wakening of things sleeping. Revealing of old things forgotten.

∽

Don't forget: "The mountains are singing, and the Lady comes."

∽

Bird Rock. The birds remember. It is the door.

∽

The "brenin bren y Ganllwyd," the great king oak near Dolgellau, felled in the early 18th century. Bole contained 609 cubic feet, and above this towered four great branches, each long enough for a mill shaft.

∽

Sandpipers run, and scoot off into the air, in pairs and tens and little flocks. One leads Will somewhere.

∽

Triad from the 13th century Exeter Chronica de Wallia: "These are the kingdoms which the sea destroyed. . . . The second kingdom was that of Henig son of Glannog; it was between Cardigan and Bardsey, and as far as St. David's. That land was very good, fertile and level, and it was called Maes Maichgen; it lay from the mouth (of the Ystwyth?) to Llyn, *and up to Aberdovey. . . .*"

ᵔ

The Doors come back, perhaps in Book Five.

ᵔ

In Welsh, "glas" can mean green as well as blue, silver, greyish-white and slate-colored. The Welsh word for "grass" is "glas-wellt" (lit. green straw).

ᵔ

"Three freights of Prydwen went we into it, But seven came back from Caer Siddi." The seventh is Arthur, and we never see him. No one does, but Merriman.

ᵔ

A sailor tattooed with a star between thumb and forefinger.

ᵔ

Bran/Herne/Arthur. Perhaps to the very last minute I shan't be sure whether he stays or goes.

ᵔ

Corona Borealis, the Crown of the North Wind, just dipping over the northern horizon at midsummer.

ᵔ

The sea level was changing in the fifth century, causing floods; same time as the Saxons were harrying the Romano-British. Irish invading too. In the peace of Arthur, the English had Sussex, Kent, Norfolk but not Bucks, Middlesex, Oxford. Twenty-one years between

Badon, and Arthur dying at "Camlann." When does
the Tree grow? Well—now, I suppose. Or outside
Time.

∾

At the last battle, Will glimpses all the lost faces:
Owain, Gwion, the king. Even a girl throwing him a red
rose. You never did use that red rose. . . .

∾

In the "Poetics" Aristotle said, "A likely impossibility
is always preferable to an unconvincing possibility." I think
those of us who write fantasy are dedicated to making impossible things seem likely, making dreams seem real. We
are somewhere between the Impressionists and abstract
painters. Our writing is haunted by those parts of our experience which we do not understand, or even consciously
remember. And if you, child or adult, are drawn to our work,
your response comes from that same shadowy land. Like us,
you are escaping into yourselves.

I have been attempting definitions, but I am never really
comfortable when writing about "fantasy." The label is so
limiting. It seems to me that every work of art is a fantasy,
every book or play, painting or piece of music, everything
that is made, by craft and talent, out of somebody's imagination. We have all dreamed, and recorded our dreams as best
we could. How can we define what we are doing? How can
a fish describe what it's like to swim?

So having asked those questions, I sat in my study
brooding hopelessly over a proper dispassionate description
of the nature of fantasy, when I heard slow careful footsteps

on the stairs. My daughter Kate came in, carrying a dish of water in one hand and some curious funnel-like instrument in the other. I said, "I'm stuck."

Kate smiled vaguely but ignored this, just as she had ignored the prohibition against Disturbing Mother at Work. She said, "Watch," and she dipped the funnel into the dish and blew through it, and out of the funnel grew the most magnificent bubble I have ever seen, iridescent, gleaming.

"Look at it from here," said Kate, intent. "Just look at the light!" And in the sunlight, all the colors in the world were swimming over that glimmering sphere—swirling, glowing, achingly beautiful. Like a dancing rainbow the bubble hung there for a long moment; then it was gone.

I thought: *That's* fantasy.

I said: "I wish they didn't have to vanish so soon."

"But you can always blow another," Kate said.

Some Thoughts on Imagination in Children's Literature

Paula Fox

Literature is the province of imagination, and stories, in whatever guise, are meditations on life.

Goethe wrote that supreme imagining is the effort to grasp truth through imagination. It does not consist in making things different but in trying to discover them as they are.

Imagination is random and elusive. We deduce its presence by its effects, just as we deduce that a breeze has sprung up, a breeze we can't see, because we hear and see the rustling of leaves in a tree. It is the guardian spirit that we sense in great stories; we feel its rustling.

Imagination can be stillborn; it can be stifled. But it can be awakened. When you read to a child, when you put a book in a child's hands, you are bringing that child news of the infinitely varied nature of life. You are an awakener.

Few have attested so passionately to the power of books as the Russian writer Maxim Gorki. As a child, he lived in a remote nineteenth-century village, Nizhni. When he was ten, he was farmed out as a servant to a provincial family. Here is how he describes it in *Childhood,* the first volume of his autobiographical trilogy:

> Those winter evenings in that little cramped room with my master and mistress were quite unbearable. Outside there was nothing but deathly night. Sometimes I could hear the frost crackling. People sat at the table, as silent as frozen fish. Sometimes a blizzard would buffet the window and the walls, roar down the chimneys and make a banging noise in the dampers. The babies would start crying in the nursery and one felt like sitting down in some dark corner, hunching oneself up and howling like a wolf.

But Gorki didn't howl like a wolf. Instead, he learned to read. And although there were very few books in that woebegone village, he managed to get hold of most of them. But he was punished for reading, and so he read secretly at night. The books, he writes,

> . . . made the world a larger place, beautifying it with fabulous towns, showing the high mountains and wonderful seashores. Life blossomed miraculously, the earth became more attractive, richer in people and towns and many different things. And now as I looked at those distant fields beyond the Volga, I knew very well they were not just a desert. . . . The earth had seemed empty and lonely. And as a result my heart became empty. . . . All desire would disappear and there would be simply nothing to think about. . . . As I read, I began to feel healthier and stronger, and I worked

rapidly and skilfully, as I now had a purpose, the sooner I finished my chores, the more time would be left over for reading. When they took books away from me, I became listless and lazy, and a morbid forgetfulness which I had not known before would take hold of me.

Gorki soon tired of stories in which there was a simpleminded, shadowless confrontation between pure good and pure evil, with evil inevitably routed and good inevitably triumphant. At ten, he knew better. He knew that good and evil were often inextricably tangled in the same person, the same event. But what had originally excited his imagination in those early fables he read was a sense of a world utterly unlike Nizhni.

Although those fantasies had begun by leading him away, out of his own life, they also had the extraordinary effect of helping him to discover his own life, as though up until then it, too, had been an unknown country beyond the Volga.

Books awakened Gorki's imagination, not only about different people and places, but about himself. And instead of "morbid forgetfulness," instead of brutish resignation, Gorki began to perceive with imaginative vision that there was more to his grandfather than his cruelty, more to his grandmother than her lunacy, and that the people of his village were not merely fools, or dangerous beasts, or drunken sots, but were, as he was, baffled and fearful and struggling to endure.

Gorki discovered another marvel about stories—their power to bring comfort to people, to divert them and make them merry, to enchant them. He found that he, himself, could invent such stories, and he told them even to those people who had jeered at him for reading. He saw that he could make them laugh, make them forget, for a little while, the meagerness of their daily lives and bring them into the realm that William Wordsworth described as: "That twilight when we first begin to see this dawning earth . . ."

The first intimations of "this dawning earth"! I do not have to make an effort to recollect how the beginning of certain books affected me when I first read them, because they still do. Such beginnings as: "Call me Ishmael." Or, "An angry man—there is my story: the bitter rancour of Achilles, Prince of the House of Peleus, which brought a thousand troubles upon the Achaian host." Or, "Alice was beginning to get very tired of sitting by her sister on the bank, and of having nothing to do. . . ." Or, "Emma Wood-house, handsome, clever, and rich, with a comfortable home and happy disposition, seemed to unite some of the best blessings of existence; and had lived nearly twenty-one years with very little to distress or vex her." Or, "Happy families are alike but an unhappy family is unhappy after its own fashion." Or, "Midway in our life's journey, I went astray from the straight road and woke to find myself alone in a dark wood."

But along with the literature of imagination, there has always been tract literature. Stories that once strained to instruct young readers in how to attain virtue and the happiness of virtue have been replaced now by stories that strain to teach children how to manage life by merely naming such "problems" as disease, physical anomalies, and even death, and assuring them there is nothing to be afraid of, nothing to suffer about, nothing complex.

Samuel Taylor Coleridge attacked the old didactic literature for its debasement of human pity and passion 190 years ago when he heard from a friend a description of a children's book typical of that period. He writes: "A child is to come home and tell its mother, 'The sixpence you gave me I gave to a beggar. Did I do right, Mamma?'—'O! yes my dear,' cries the mother, kissing him, 'you did,'—thus blending one of the first virtues, charity, with one of the basest passions of the human heart, the love of hearing oneself praised."

And Coleridge goes on to say, "[I] sought no praise for giving to beggars, and I trust that my heart is not the worse, or the less inclined to feel sympathy for all men, because I first learnt the powers of my nature, and to reverence that nature—for who can feel and reverence the nature of man and not feel deeply for the afflictions of others possessing like powers and like nature?"

Recently, I saw a letter an acquaintance received from a television producer of programs for children that suggests the fashion of the new didacticism. In turning down my acquaintance's book for television adaptation, the producer wrote that it was a "superior" work, but that it did not "fall into the rigid guidelines set forth by our network personnel," who, said the producer, are now "tending toward crisis stories . . . concerning diabetics, suicides, teenage pregnancies, etc."

The "etc." speaks powerfully of the way in which the most profound and painful difficulties of living have become trivialized.

A choice of subject matter has never made writing. And it has not been the function of literature to show people of any age how to deal with problems or how to solve social and sexual dilemmas. The implicit instructions of contemporary "realistic" books may vary from those of 1810, but they have the same sequel: they smother speculation, they stifle uncertainty, they strangle imagination.

It is difficult to believe the authors of such books, of any era, believe that children possess "like powers and like nature," to be reverenced, to be respected. They are rather like W. H. Auden's social worker: "Writers can be guilty of every kind of human conceit but one, the conceit of the social worker," he writes, then goes on to characterize his social worker's view of life: "We are all here on earth to help others: what on earth the others are here for, I don't know."

I suggest that if, in literature, we are given nothing to think about, to imagine, outside the external trappings of our own lives, we are likely to remain motionless and ignorant. And the earth will, indeed, seem empty and lonely as it was to Gorki when he was deprived of books.

We are all born provincials, but there is in us that push against the constraint of circumstances, of the given, that we show in our first efforts to stand up on legs that are not quite ready to support us, in that struggle toward a larger life we make in our first attempts at human speech.

If we make the effort, the imaginative effort, we can sometimes see the inherent imaginative energy in a child's astonishment at fire, at thunder, at birds and cats and wheels, at colors and shapes and the texture and taste of things—at all, in fact, which is always in peril of becoming commonplace to us because we are "grown-ups" and because we have ceased to venerate life, and have "solved" its puzzles.

Any passing observations of infancy and growth can

tell us about the discomfort and joy of being alive, sorrow and joy, bound together from the beginning.

But often we want to forget, to swathe our seminal awareness in comfort. And we present children with cozy books about divorce and desertion and death and sex, promising them that, in the end, everything can be made all right. Thus we drown eternal human questions with contemporary bromides, all mechanics and sanctimony, filled with a ruinous complacency.

Just as junk food can dull pangs of hunger, so can junk books dull the hunger of a child's mind, stuff it with unearned certainties, those straws, Henry James wrote, that "we chew to cheat our appetites."

A characteristic of such literature is that it tends to promote and vindicate adult predispositions toward children and childhood. Another is that these books deliver us from the responsibility, the effort of self-knowledge without which we cannot really think about and understand children, who are not a race apart but ourselves when new.

But the truths we sense in great imaginative literature send us back to the earliest, most essential memories of our own lives, and, at the same time, direct our vision outward toward other lives, toward life itself.

I was taught to read when I was five. The old house where I lived in those days was filled with books and not much else. The roof leaked, the well was always going dry, the wallpaper peeled, the furniture was patched and mended, the driveway up the long hill to the house was impassable in heavy rain or snow, and there was never enough money for repairs.

But the books! They lined the walls of the rooms; they

stood in columns on the floor; they were piled up in the attic on top of a river of *National Geographics* that cascaded down the crowded attic stairs.

In bad weather, when I couldn't go outside, I used to sit on those stairs and extract a *Geographic* as carefully as if I were playing pick-up-sticks, so I wouldn't bring the whole attic down on myself. Among the glossy pages of the magazines, I met up with pygmies and Balinese dancers, cities built on water, mountain peaks yet unscaled, desert people and people who lived amid eternal snow, dragonflies and anacondas. On those attic stairs in an old house that seemed always on the verge of collapse, I began to sense huge possibilities.

Some years later, I went to live on a sugar plantation in the middle of Cuba—a far distance from an old Victorian wreck on the Hudson River! I had no books there except for one or two ragged textbooks passed among the students, of which I was one, whose school was one room attached to the rear of a small church. Still, there was a man who came to our village once a month from the city of Cienfuegos. He came on one of the dusty roads that led to the plantation, pushing a handcart in front of him. In it were piles of two-sheet "books" that reproduced songs that were current and popular in Havana. The paper, I recall, was a harsh and acid pink. The sheets were so poorly printed that sometimes whole lines were blotted out. A child would buy a few pages for a *centavo* or two and I, along with the other children of the plantation, would memorize all the words and sing them to each other. Some of the songs told real stories with beginnings and middles and ends, stories that were often sad, but comic now and then, too. One, I remember, was about a

garbage man whose sweetheart deserted him, and he grew
so melancholy, he lost all interest in his work! That particular song had the lyrical title *El Cantino Arabal.* Such was our
longing for stories that we made up still others of our own,
inventing for ourselves a kind of mythology of which those
coarse pink sheets of paper were the text.

When I returned to the United States, I went to live in
a small community on Long Island. A few other little girls
and I found an abandoned shed in the neighborhood and
decided to start our own library. We pooled our books, and
somewhere we dug up a few sticks of furniture. Until the
cold drove us out, along with the awful depredations of a
neighborhood gang of small boys who regarded us as enemies, we spent many charmed hours after school in our
library. By the time we had to abandon it, I had a real library
card.

When I was in the seventh grade, we had to memorize
a good deal of poetry, especially William Wordsworth's poetry. No one I knew then, except a born actor or two, really
liked to memorize poems. It was hard work. But we did it.
And the poems stayed in my mind, within reach for many
years. As I got older, I began to read poetry for my own
pleasure, and among the poets who seemed to me to be
magician-saints, Wordsworth towered, difficult, dense, as
remote and unimaginable a human being as Pericles.

A few years ago, I spent some weeks in the Lake Country in England. I went to visit Dove Cottage where Wordsworth and his family lived from 1800 to 1808. It was a
clenched little house full of dark passages and tiny rooms.
In the kitchen, there was a black, rusted coffee grinder the
Wordsworths had used. I could hardly tear my glance from

it. It had never occurred to me that Wordsworth had been real!

Later, I went on to Rydal Hall, a few miles away from Grasmere. It was a lovely Georgian house Wordsworth had rented when he became a little prosperous. It stood on a hill, and all around it were his gardens, just as he had planted them. The house had only recently returned to the Wordsworth descendants. Two elderly women from Grasmere kept guard over it and took the few pence it cost to explore it.

As I passed by one of them, she whispered something to me. I leaned forward. More loudly, she said, "Miss Wordsworth! She's in there!" And she pointed to a narrow door next to her chair.

I thought she was speaking of a ghost. I nodded. She smiled. "His great-great-granddaughter," she explained.

At that moment, the narrow door crashed open into the little hall where I stood, and out came a large, handsome middle-aged woman in a fierce tweed suit. A cigarette drooped from her lips, and she was smiling with immense good humor. I was introduced. She shook my hand vigorously and asked, "Are you enjoying the house?"

I don't remember what I replied. I do remember that I remained rooted to the spot as she swept out the front door, hurled herself into a dilapidated station wagon, reversed violently, knocked into a fence, laughed, waved to me out the car window, cigarette ashes flying, and disappeared down the driveway.

It is not memory alone, but imagination that brings back to me the palpable presence of that car-banging, tweedy woman, her amiable face afloat in the smoke of her

The Art
of Realism

❧

Jill Paton Walsh

It is famous that Plato ordained that poets—that is to say, writers of fiction—should be crowned with laurel, and turned away from the gates of the ideal republic because they told lies.

In our time one kind of fiction—fantasy—has usually been singled out for attack on the grounds of untruth more often than other kinds. As a result, for it has many admirers and many talented practitioners, fantasy has been very eloquently defended. The trouble is that the defense of fantasy is often made at the expense of what is usually called realism. A claim, for example, that fantasy is the best, or even the only tool for exploring inner reality, may well seem to be implying that a book in the realistic mode can explore only outer reality, and cannot plumb much psychological depth.

So the first point one must make about realism is that it, too, is fantasy. Realistic fiction is about imaginary people, living in imagined contexts, doing what was never done, saying what was never said. Plato did not make distinctions between one kind of liar and another, but sent the lot packing together! Some people believe that *more* imagination is required to write fantasy, but I do not believe that. A great deal of imagination is required to write anything, and give it breathing life; compared to the amount required to work the trick at all, any increase in the amount required to do dragons as compared to mailmen is trivial.

Before going further I had perhaps better make it clear that it is as a writer that I am a critic. In writing about realism I am not concerned with defending any particular books to which that term applies, least of all my own, and I am not attacking books of fantasy. I am meditating on the possibilities of those forms, and if I am defending anything it is the idea that writing a work of realistic fiction for young readers is a worthwhile enterprise for a writer to embark upon.

Of course, the easiest justification of such writing is the extent of the demand for it. "Realism," especially if it is felt to have a quality known as "relevance," is of the greatest possible interest to teachers and librarians, and every writer must have been made to feel so. Especially in the U.S.A., works of realism predominate in numbers and acclaim on the children's list. And yet this is not entirely comforting from the writer's point of view, even if she is going to write exactly the kind of thing that seems to be in favor. That is because of the ambiguous nature of the approval of realism.

Books for children are often wanted rather simplistically for their content. People working with children in slums want books about children in slums. When they do they almost always think in terms of realistic treatments of slums and slum children. So many of those who work with children ask writers for books like these that I suppose we should defer to experience and accept that children do find books that are recognizable easier to like and read. I say that I suppose we should accept this, though some of my own experience points against accepting it. I recall on a visit to Darlington, a few years back, being asked by the adults I met for books about ordinary children living in bleak industrial towns like Darlington, books that their pupils and borrowers would understand. But the children in Darlington, rather more tactfully than the adults, also suggested to me books I might like to write for them. "Have you ever thought of writing a pony book?" one of them asked. And another said, "Couldn't you write a book about witches and magic? I like witches." A third said, "I liked the bit in your book about the sea. I've never seen the sea. Holidays we always go to our gran's in Ashbourne." I take it that two of these children wanted realism, and one wanted fantasy, and none wanted relevance to Darlington. I realize that they might none the less have liked it if they got it.

A related demand calls for books that will directly confront the problems of states of childhood and adolescence; books about where the reader is emotionally rather than geographically. Here, too, it is noticeable that a work of fantasy is seldom regarded as a suitable answer to the request.

I think this is because fantasy compels a kind of literary reading—in adults, I mean. The way children read is a mystery and an astonishment to me, and I do not want to offer generalizations about it. But in the nature of things many people become deeply concerned with children's reading— parents, for example, or those nonspecialists who teach children early in life, and whose own original interests may have lain in the sciences rather than the arts—who are not necessarily literary people. If a book has a dragon in it, then maybe one dismisses it as rubbish (and of course that reaction is not unheard of, and is one of the things that has brought into being the defense of fantasy as better, deeper, more imaginative, etc., etc.). But if you do not instantly dismiss the book as rubbish, you do have to read it in a ranging way, seeking a metaphorical meaning, or many such meanings. There are no dragons in the world; but there are ferocious, greedy and destructive keepers of goldhoards. And there is greed in one's own soul. A work of fantasy compels a reader into a metaphorical frame of mind. A work of realism, on the other hand, permits very literal-minded readings, even downright stupid ones. It allows itself to be read as if fictions were simple, one-horse rides, with only one drift, one meaning. It allows people to make neat little extracts of the "moral" of the story, and then to think of another moral for which they would like a story, and go looking for that. Even worse, it is possible to read a realistic book as though it were not really fiction at all, but a statement of fact of some kind—a narrative chunk of autobiography, reminiscence, eyewitness account, or some such.

The readers of these books may find that hard to believe. But all writers of realism can tell you how often they have been asked if what they have written was based on their own life. Of course, what one has written is based on one's own life—what else could it be based on?—but the questioner means "Did this happen to you?" Once, when in the interests of a more subtle truth I told an audience that I was all the girl characters I had written, in some way or

Another thing that seems often to be forgotten when realism is being discussed is that fiction, by its nature, is general. Too often a quest is mounted for books that will be "relevant" in the sense that they will contain workouts of the very same problems the readers may have, in the same circumstances. On this question I have a carefully considered opinion; and since it runs counter to the requests of many people experienced in working with children, I would like to point out that my view, too, is based on experience —experience as a writer, which includes meetings with many hundreds of children, and many hundreds of those who work with them, hundreds of letters from readers, and many, many hours of engagement with the difficulties of my craft. I think that though it is possible to learn from books of fiction, it is not possible to teach with them; though it is possible for a book to heal psychic wounds, it is not possible to use books for the practice of psychic medicine. And the reason for this is the quirky, various, and totally unpredictable nature of the individual reaction to a book. I am constantly astonished at the temerity of those who are certain that they know just *what* in a book would help or interest children in some particular state of mind, or growth, or difficulty. I have certainly never known my own children as well as that, affectionate and happy as my dealings with them and from them have been, and deeply though I have been preoccupied with them. For to know with whom readers will identify in a book you have to know how they see themselves. That will often not be how we see them. A pathetic, waif sort of child from a poor family may not readily see herself as pathetic; she may not see herself at all as the child in the slum story written with her in mind; she may latch on with glee to Elizabeth Bennett, being cheeky to the aristocracy. In order to use a book to help someone, you have to foresee what their reaction to the book will be.

I believe reactions to fiction to be unforeseeable, and manipulation with fiction, including manipulation for the person's own good, to be not so much inartistic and impertinent, as impossible. I would except rare flashes of intuition, between friends. For one does sometimes guess, correctly, that such-and-such a person would like this book.

While we are thinking about the application of books to readers, I would like to point out how this particular brokerage seems to be conducted only with children's books; one does not rush to give *Anna Karenina* to friends who are committing adultery, or minister to distressed old age with copies of *King Lear.*

So I would say that a literary treatment of some problem is not good because it may directly apply to some children, but good if it can engage the interests of a very large number of children, most of whom will not find themselves in the exact dilemmas described. A problem book is good enough for the child with the problem only if it is good enough for everybody else. Literature works not by being particular, but by being general.

Of course, what I am saying now bears on the question of the relationship between the children's writer and her readers. I write the kind of books that not infrequently bring me letters of personal appeal for advice or consolation or moral support. I answer them as best I can. I am sometimes baffled, flattered, and touched that a reader thinks of asking me for help. But an important act of friendship was performed by writing the best book I could in the first place. The relationship of a writer to a reader is not that of parent or therapist, and it will not bear particularized nurturing; it is not that of a teacher to a pupil, and it will not bear the weight of deliberate teaching; it is not that of preacher to congregation, and it will not bear sermonizing. It is the relationship of willing listener to loving narrator. An unforced voluntariness on the part of the reader is a necessary part of it; a disinterested desire to tell a story for its own sake and let it have what effect it will is the writer's part.

I cannot say that much of the welcome for books of realism on the children's list is off-key, from the writer's viewpoint, without facing the obvious retort: Why, in that case, work on the children's list at all? Unlike the writer of fantasy, pushed by publishing convention into a kind of nature-reserve children's corner, the writer of realism could easily write for adults and deal with a wider and more mature appreciation of the real world that he is so keen to embody in literature.

The answer I would give is that the nature of my subjects makes my approach appropriate. I am fascinated by the relationship of child and adult, and most of all the process —never completed, always in critical stages of advance and change—by which one becomes the other. This subject has often been explored in adult literature, to the point of having become a cliché. In hundreds of novels and biographies and autobiographies the disillusionments and corruptions, or even the triumphs and redemptions of growth, have been celebrated, in retrospect. To set oneself back behind the process, in the position children find themselves in, and explore it in prospect or in process seems at least as interesting a thing to do. Maturing is accomplished by every human being, not in retrospect, but by stumbling forward.

I think that it is often felt that a child's view of reality is not really important, because it is transitory. And of course it is true that in each human life a child's viewpoint is of limited duration, and is outgrown and modified in many ways, not all of them improvements in the quality of perception, but most of them in the right direction. But in the life of humanity the viewpoint of the young is not transitory. As fast as you or I grew out of it, it was replenished by others, younger than us. In a constantly changing group of children it is always with us, always to be lived with, envied, argued with, changed. And adult writers can, of course, simply look down in retrospect from where they are now; or they can use their elongated perspective to go back, and then edge forward. It is as much an aspect of reality that at any time many people are young and apt to see the world like this, as it is that at any time many people are older and sadder and wiser; and fiction can as well be used to meditate on the one as the other.

The youth of the reader is a mysterious, challenging element in the inspiration of the writer. The world is made new by it. There is also the new inhabitant's need for mind-maps with which to begin to learn and explore the world. Now, although there are dangers in the world for which dragons may function as symbols, there are no dragons. There are states of mind in the world for which dragons work as analogs, but there are no dragons. The dragon offers the writer a chance to embody depths of meaning, but strips it of particular reference. Is Tolkien's Mordor, Hitler's Germany? Any State corrupted by power? The Christian Hell? All of these? To understand the dragon you need a grasp both of symbol *and* of actuality. The complex, stubborn, chaotic real world is, in the end, the subject of any kind of book.

I am a devoted Realist, with only one book of fantasy

Forever Pedaling on the Road to Realism

∾

Robert Cormier

I am riding the bicycle and I am on Route 13 in Leominster, Massachusetts, on my way to Lake Whalom and I am pedaling furiously, although this is a ten-speed bike with all the latest paraphernalia. A beautiful bike—the kind I never rode as a kid, but that my daughter takes for granted because she doesn't remember the old-fashioned bikes with balloon tires, without gears, and brakes that didn't always work. It's hot as I pedal along, the heat invading my pores and sinking into my bones, and I squint my eyes against the dying sun. My muscles ache and my eyes sting. But I keep pedaling, I keep pedaling.

This is Main Street in Leominster and to my right is Barone's Drug Store, where my daughter—not the daughter who owns the bike but another one—worked as a clerk during high school. I glance at the place and think of this daughter and her home in Scituate on the seacoast and of her upcoming visit here to Leominster. It's six-thirty in the evening and it is summer, a James Agee kind of summer, like the one he writes about in *A Death in the Family*—summer dusk after supper when he describes the men hosing their lawns and one man whose shirt is fishlike pale in the light and his face nearly anonymous. Nobody seems to read James Agee anymore, not anyone I know, at least. But I forget about James Agee because I am approaching Our Lady of the Lake Church and I have to concentrate now on the pedaling because the roadway inclines sharply and my legs begin to throb with pain. I see a kid walking along on the sidewalk and I wave at him and he doesn't see me and doesn't wave back. . . .

What's going on here, anyway?

A spoof of the opening of *I Am the Cheese?*

Or an attempt at parody?

Neither, really.

The above paragraphs describe what actually happened one evening recently when my thirteen-year-old daughter enticed me into a bike ride after supper. I had been rereading James Agee and his marvelous description of summer evenings in Knoxville, Tennessee, and his words echoed in me as I pedaled, ignoring the protest of my bones. During the ride I also pondered the nature of realism in adolescent fiction in preparation for an article I planned to write on the subject. It occurred to me that I was doing the same thing Adam Farmer had done in the opening pages of *I Am the Cheese,* thinking the same kind of thoughts, pedaling uncertainly the same way Adam had pedaled. My ride, of course, was actual while Adam's was fictional, existing only on the printed page. But did that make Adam's ride any less real? Thus reality, or, rather, the illusion of reality. But what of realism, which is something altogether different? If Adam in the novel had ridden off into the sunset with his beloved Amy Hertz beside him and Mr. Grey left behind in defeat, then the novel would probably have been described as a romantic adventure. But Adam had taken no sunset ride to freedom and Amy Hertz had disappeared somewhere and Mr. Grey had emerged triumphant, if somewhat tarnished, and thus *I Am the Cheese* is cited as an example of realism in novels for young readers. But does an unhappy ending alone make a novel realistic?

The strange thing is that I am more concerned with reality than realism in the novels I write, despite the evidence of *The Chocolate War, I Am the Cheese,* and *After the First Death.* Realism is a label other people have applied to the novels. Labels are also applied after the fact. What counts is the writing itself, what happens before the fact. For a long time, I was reluctant to analyze my writing and grew uncomfortable when I encountered articles arguing certain aspects of it, the quality of realism, say, in *The Chocolate War.* I felt like one of those characters in a television cartoon who flies through the air until he becomes conscious of what he's doing and looks down in horror, loses the ability to fly, and plummets to the earth. Too much theorizing worries me. It makes me too conscious of the nuts and bolts of writing. It makes me feel as though I am looking into a mirror as I write.

Why look into the mirror, then?

Blame the letters. The letters began it all.

Dear Mr. Cormier:

I have just finished reading your book, *The Chocolate War.* I enjoyed it very much. But the ending to your book surprised me. I expected Jerry Renault to win the fight against Emile Janza or to at least regain his respect with all the guys in the school. Why did Jerry lose?

When these letters first began to arrive—most of them from junior-high or high-school students—I was both puzzled and somewhat put off by the questions. I wanted to answer the letters or at least acknowledge them. If a reader cares enough to sit down and write a letter after finishing a novel, then certainly the author owes the reader an answer. Yet, answering the questions seemed an act of defense. Why should the writer be placed in the position of defending what he writes? The novel itself should stand alone. I found myself answering the letters, however, and explaining . . .

> Dear Kathy:
> I sympathize with you about the unhappy ending of the novel and the fact that Jerry Renault did not win in the end. But I was trying to write realistically even though I knew it would upset some people. The fact is that the good guys don't always win in real life and I wanted to show that. I also wanted to indict those who don't try to help, who remain indifferent in the face of evil or wrongdoing. They are as bad as or probably worse than the villain themselves. . . .

I hope the answer satisfied Kathy. I hope all the answers I have written satisfied all the readers who wrote letters. But I am still somewhat unsatisfied myself. Because, frankly, my original purpose in writing the novels was different from what I cited in the letters. First, I sought reality, not realism. I wanted to bring to life people like Jerry Renault and Adam Farmer and poor Tubs Casper, who appears for only one poignant moment, and I wanted to make the reader feel the mounting heat and pressure in that hijacked bus while a child trembled in the night. These were my first concerns. And if that worked, then I indulged myself in the philosophical aspects of the novel—the exploration of themes, the investigation of the do-your-own-thing philosophy, the plight of the individual against society, the possibility of innocence as evil, not only *masked* as evil but evil itself. But first came the emotions and then the characters. Once the characters are created and they become as real to you as the people you stand in line with at the movies that night, you must follow the inevitability of their actions. These actions determine the course and outcome of the novel.

Following that procedure with *The Chocolate War,* I woke up one day to find myself hailed as a proponent of realism in adolescent fiction. As if I had staked out this territory for myself. As if I were some kind of pioneer. I felt like an imposter and still do. I am a writer who is simply trying to be honest in the practice of my craft. I am no expert on realism in the modern novel. I am expert only about my own work and nobody else's. That is why I write about my own work when asked to put down thoughts about writing. Yet, if the history of the individual repeats the history of the race, then perhaps the thoughts of one writer reflects the thoughts of some other writers.

Another letter:

Dear Mr. Cormier:
I have read your three novels and, in fact, just finished *After the First Death* a few minutes ago. I am still shattered. Why do you always have to write unhappy

endings? It seems to me you are deliberately doing this.
Why couldn't Kate have escaped? As the writer, you
had it in your power to let Kate get away. Why didn't
you?

I received this letter shortly before a publishing house
asked me to write an article about my "unhappy endings"
for its newsletter. Perhaps the thoughts in that article, incorporated here, provide a glimpse at least into the workings of
reality and realism in one specific novel.

It must be pointed out immediately that the characters
in my novels are very much real persons to me, and as real
persons they take on independent lives of their own. Kate
Forrester in *After the First Death* is an example of what I mean.

I had always wanted to write about that lovely all-
American girl we all know. She causes our heads to turn
when she strolls down the street. She's the cheerleader who
always has a date for the big prom, the girl who is always
chosen for the lead in the senior class play. Blonde, slender,
beautiful, almost a cliché. Yet we know that behind the
facade there lurks a person. What kind of person, really?
Obviously, not perfect, simply because no human being is
perfect. She has weaknesses, doubts, and defects. What
would happen if this girl, with her beauty and flaws, were
placed in a position of stress? How would she react? I didn't
know the answer to that last question when I first introduced Kate, but I knew that her reactions would have to ring
true: she would have to act according to her character,
strengths, and weaknesses, and not be moved around like a
chess piece on a board.

As the events in *After the First Death* unfolded, Kate Forrester turned out to be stronger and more courageous than I had anticipated. Yet, her entire life prior to the crisis in the novel had not prepared her for the role she had to play. Her self-doubts always remained, providing a poignance I had not foreseen. She was brave, all right, but she constantly doubted her capacity to be brave. Another thing: her courage led her to take risks. Would it eventually lead her to an overwhelming and miscalculated risk? I didn't know. (Frankly, by this time, I was madly in love with Kate Forrester and wished her only the best.) But I knew that what happened to her would be the inevitable result of who and what she was and the events in which she was caught.

The important word here is *inevitable.* I always yield to the inevitability of events in my novels even when it causes me to shift courses, toss away pages and notes, and make sudden revisions. The novels that fail to satisfy me as a reader are those in which I sense the writer manipulating his characters, going against the grain of character and event to achieve a calculated ending. A happy ending attached to a novel whose flow and tone and development is downbeat fatally flaws the work.

As I began *After the First Death,* I thought that at last I might be embarking on the love story I had been wanting to write. I also thought a happy ending was entirely possible. Kate was attractive and appealing. The boy Miro, who confronts her on that fateful bus, seemed ready for an emotional explosion. In the confinement of the bus, their protective layers torn off by the crisis, their emotions accelerated by the swift events, I thought it possible that the boy and girl could fall in love. As they began to know each other, as events began to strip them of their defenses, emotional collisions did take place. But the outcome was not the love story I had envisioned.

The letter I quoted claims that the writer has it in his power to alter the course of a character's life. Yes, but . . . Kate and Miro could have fallen in love, Miro could have awakened to the humanity within that he had been denying, and Kate could have escaped without harm, but it would not have been true to the events, the tone, the dramatic fore-shadowing. And, I believe, the sense of inevitability would have been missing.

This sense of inevitability is perhaps the dominant fac-tor. It is perfectly caught in a scene that haunts me, from one of the many movies depicting the sinking of the *Titanic.* The ship has struck the iceberg, panic is rampant, water is flowing into the bowels of the vessel. An engineer assesses the damage, calculates the rate of water pouring into the ship, all the checks and balances. At last, he reports to the captain: the ship must go down. Must. Not *may* sink or *will* sink but *must* sink as the ship obeys a law as immutable as a mathematical truth.

This kind of situation confronted me one evening when I had reached the midway point of *After the First Death.* I realized with a kind of horror that one of the child hostages —at least one—must be killed in cold blood as a retaliatory measure by the terrorists. I didn't want that to happen. I paced the floor as if I were on a picket line protesting my own novel. One child had already died accidentally near the beginning of the book. Another death? In cold blood? It would be terrible to write and terrible to read. I considered the situation: the hijacked bus surrounded by hundreds of soldiers and police officers and, in particular, snipers; helicopters wheeling in the air; pressure building up inside and outside the bus as the hours passed; the weariness; the itchy trigger fingers. It seemed not only likely but inevitable that someone would miscalculate, a trigger finger would twitch, a nerve would leap, an irrevocable mistake would be made. And a child would die—must die—just as the foundering ship must sink in obedience to an unavoidable law.

And yet. And yet.

I am still looking for a happy ending. I envision Amy Hertz and Jerry Renault meeting and falling in love in Monument, Amy having returned from a vacation abroad and Jerry having recovered in mind and spirit after that beating at Trinity High. I ponder the possibility of Archie Costello's luck running out the year he graduates from college, the outside world turning him into a victim finally, the black marble turning up at last. And what of Adam Farmer? Ah, Adam. I see him pedaling his bike to freedom, the wind in his hair, his mind clear of drugs and serums, his horizons no longer lost. And his identity as Paul Delmonte intact at last.

Isn't that beautiful to contemplate?

But not realistic, sad to say.

Changing Woman, Working

∾

Virginia Hamilton

It is place and time that are close to the heart of so many
of my fictions. The *place* is a minuscule, unlikely piece of
midwestern America where I was born, which made a profound impression. I was all of nine when I realized I could
not be for long without the hot, wet, whelming scent of
fresh-mown green grass on the oppression of August. The
time would be that period of my early life transformed and
heightened to uniqueness through the creative process; or it
is the memory of my life, or my mother's memory of her life
as told to me, revised by me; or that of her mother's and her
grandmother's and her old friends. Time and place are
bound together, no longer real; yet, they remain a solid
sensation in the present of that which has been accomplished. The longer I remain in this small village, my time
and place in Ohio, the more deeply I comprehend it as the
source for all of the fiction I create.

There is no glamour for me in the sight of distant places,
although I enjoy exploring them. My subject matter is

derived from the intimate and shared place of the hometown and the hometown's people, and all that is known and remembered and imagined through time over time therefrom.

Here, I find my emotional landscape as well as the geographical location for the stories. Time and place are so very important to my spiritual self. For I have suffered through them in the same sense that the black people have suffered through them toward freedom. The progress of the people across the hopescape of America gives to my writing a sense of continuity and a narrative drama—the spiritual impact called style—so important to any writer.

In my daily life, I see myself not at all as a writer but as a woman working, a day laborer. Hidden behind the picture, I suppose, is still the unfocused vision of the writer that compelled me in the beginning, that of the humble crusader locked in the garret room, suffering for life, "creating" all-purpose prose with bruised, delicate hands. So important to that vision were those below on the ground, who, looking to the garret window, whispered in awe, "There lives the *author!*"

The truth is, the work I do is a long haul day after day from the beginning of a fiction to its end. I never lack for beginnings of fictions. What I do lack at first is the knowledge of the process for discovering the art form that will transform ideas into coherent fictions. It is a challenge for me to come to terms with the stunning revelation that there is no way of knowing beforehand how a fiction is to be written. One discovers how it is done only by writing it. And when it's finished, one can say to one's self, "Ah, so that's the way!"

The work I do is the only occupation I know in which acquired knowledge cannot be applied. What is learned about writing a single fiction is hopelessly inadequate in writing the next, or any others, for that matter. Each book is like a new system that must be uncovered. And realizing that I will have to find the system of it each time I begin is what keeps me startled, awake, through bleary-eyed mornings.

Each day, I labor through apprehensions, sometimes crying out, "This time, I'm not going to make it!"

But, of course, I do find the way through. If a concept occurs to me, so must its creative development follow. Therein lie instinct and intuition; solving is the natural tendency of writers. Yet, to paraphrase T. S. Eliot, between the idea and the reality falls the shadow. In the shadow, the woman working lives. In the shadow, she finds life long enough and worth the time. In the shadow, she recalls, reconstructs. I create. I am the shadow.

This, then, is not a play-pretty to be held, soft and cuddly, in the hands of the child. My fictions for children, young people, descend directly from the progress of black adults and their children across the American hopescape. Specifically, they derive from my eccentric family, from that Perry progenitor—Grandpaw Levi Perry. Levi's hand burned shut from a fire in a gunpowder mill where he slaved, three dollars a week. And the rest of his life, his hand was a fist raised high, scars hidden in its closed palm, so that the child I was might swing on it, squealing with delight. For me, ever after, the raised black fist was my Grandpaw Levi holding me on high, lifting me, higher and higher. At one time or another, it held all of my brothers and sisters on high. All of us, held high, until our legs were long enough to reach the dust where we stood on our own. And Grandpaw Perry *is* John Henry and High John de Conquer. He is inextricably bound in me with the myth of the self-made, and the closed fist of burn scars, hidden.

I believe in what I write for young people, that its call is important—the call being the essence of the people's lives [life] it depicts—and that the depiction is necessary, as well as art. In truth, I write for myself in the sense that what I write is what I care about and what pleases me, whether I make a living at it or not. I write in the hopes that my own children will have something of value and that I will have given all children something I can be proud of.

I am convinced that it is important to reveal that the life of the people is and always has been different in a significant respect from the life of the majority. It has been made eccentric by slavery, escape, fear of capture; by discrimination and constant despair. But it has held tight within it happiness, a subtle humor, a fierce pride in leadership and progress, love of life and family, and a longing for peace and freedom. Nevertheless, there is an uneasy, ideological difference with the American majority basic to black thought.

A British critic wrote about this woman working: "There is a difference in the furniture of her writing mind from that of most of her white contemporaries: dream, myth, legend and ancient story can be sensed again and again in the background of naturalistically described present-day events."[1]

That difference is directly derived from my heritage. It is the dream of freedom tantalizingly out of reach that makes the difference. A dream juxtaposed with the myth and historical truth of our proud and ancient kingdoms and their highly developed institutions and arts. Thus, our collective unconscious is set apart. And we have two consciouses: one, contemporary, and one, ancient. We are American black and we are African, to say nothing of the European strains. We infer the African; we know it was and no longer is. But we wish for it; we are bound by it and it is hauntingly imagined again and again throughout our folklore and literature.

Echoes of long past times serve to feed my imagination. They may sound of African dreams or my own family truths. Most often, they are of family. Poor we were and isolated, deliberately, surely, into clans of relatives in a remote corner of Ohio. My own family group must have been encompassed by a dream out of a Faulknerian night. We were all refined daydreamers. I was a sophisticated "nightmarer" like my father. My old man, the kind, sensitive musician, had spectacular, dangerous, also comic, nightmares that shot him out of bed and nearly out of the window with a howl and roar that could wake the lifeless. Farmers close enough to be awakened by the noise blinked a couple of times and then went back to sleep. They were my Uncle Willie and Uncle King, who realized it was Dad still trying to catch his ship that had come in.

That was Dad's favorite expression—"I'm waitin' for my ship—'lil black-hulled beauty with white trim." The nightmare commenced with Dad reaching the dock on the day of the ship's arrival, just in time. But Dad would be waylaid by The Faceless One, who pursued him throughout his hallucinatory sleep. Dad's imaginary pursuer never caught him, that I know of; yet, it caused Dad to miss his ship each time. The reason why, I suppose, my dad was a musician, composing rink-a-tink mandolin tunes and classical melodies at dawn.

I inherited the pursuer and it's a shame that Dad never learned my trick of maneuvering out of its way. I rose above it. When The Faceless One appeared out of nowhere, I flapped my arms and, miraculously, floated over its head. The thing must have comprehended defeat, for it did not last long in my sleep, perhaps a year of recurrent nightmares. I worked my arms—such will and determination that took! I didn't see a ship that had come in; but, there was an immense golden sun wafting serene on the night as I lifted off, flapping my arms. I was a child of the sun and I became a writer, I suspect, at the moment my imagination saw to my rise above the pursuer.

In the use of imagination, I am a practical working woman. My regimen is not strict; I have none of the angst that is the complaint of so many writers. Something occurs to my imagination just about every day and so I work each morning until tension develops inside me. Then, I know it's time to do something else. I take care of things here at home; and, I take care of Mother, who is eighty-eight and feisty.

It surprises me, though, that most of the time I think about making books only when I'm at the typewriter. The rest of the time, I'm living and maybe that is the key. The woman working is the woman living her life. The life energy —the humdrum, the exciting moments, the trials and tribulations, memory, knowing, imagining—serves as enrichment of the work the woman finds she is compelled to do. I work no more than five hours at a stretch. The required energy and the concentration does not last for a longer length of time.

A book, working, is hard. Yet, it is marvelous work,

surprising in that it has its own dynamism. I may begin with a fairly clear concept of story, but somewhere in the midst of it the story no longer belongs to me. It is taken over by the characters who must live it, who are individuals who change and shape it according to their own will. The created characters have their own power of intent on the page and I may not alter it to suit myself. In the early work, I did tend to exaggerate physical traits or quirks of characters. Think of Zeely Tayber's (from *Zeely*) six-and-a-half-foot height, her thin, beanpole body. Or Mr. Pluto *(The House of Dies Drear)*, his lame leg and green eyes. And Junior Brown *(The Planet of Junior Brown)*, drowning in his hugely fat body. These grotesqueries seemed necessary in order to shed light on the characters' inner life and condition. But now, my characters have few manifestations of this type, since they are constructed from the inside out from the beginning. Emotions and how they act upon them tend to reveal who the characters are. Jack Sun Run *(Arilla Sundown)*, barechested and golden, riding his horse, is a still shot, an old, sepia print, and a revelation of Jack's committment to being Amerind.

In the more recent psychic fantasy books of the *Justice Cycle (Justice and Her Brothers, Dustland* and *The Gathering)*, the extrasensory ability of telepathy and telekinesis the children have are not mere peculiarities, but represent a majestic change in the human race. Moreover, they symbolize the author's style as a signature of belief that change is what is worthy of one's concentrated effort; that the only certainty is uncertainty. Thus, the work is continually growing, changing its entertainment, as the woman working grows and changes. Changing woman, working.

My daily life does not often enter into my working. It serves better as the center of me within myself. I enjoy my life extremely; yet, I live it with a sense of melancholy, which has its origin in black history and life in America. The melancholy sense is an inherent quality of the work, inseparable from the lives of the characters. It pervades the fictional hopescape with a reality: black life is at once better and worse than it has ever been. Better for some, worse for most. This is not bitterness, it is truth.

The challenge for the woman working is to deal with the truth through youth literature with an evolvement of a fiction of compassion, love, hope, and humor. It is beyond question that as many of the young as possible should appreciate and share in the truth. For it is not mere subject matter that occasionally turns grim. It is the history of a people and their life at present. What can be shared of it is its depiction as serious entertainment through the art of children's literature.

Within the life-force of black history and traditional lore are boundless possibilities for creative work. I mean not to perpetuate a literature of despair, but to present to youth an indication of a people's range and unique capacity for living. It sounds more difficult than it is. But it is subtle work and cannot be accomplished as simply as other kinds of work with less historical grounding. On the surface, the stories are simple and straightforward. But beneath, there may be more than one meaning introduced at once. Children should not concern themselves with "understanding" the fictions in a hard and fast sense. I suggest that the best way to read is to open the mind and enjoy. Allow fiction to happen to the senses and find happiness. I do.

1. John Rowe Townsend, *A Sounding of Storytellers* (London: Kestrel Books, 1979), p.100.

Ruthie Britten and Because I Can

∽

E. L. Konigsburg

If I had gone to a school where Ruthie Britten wasn't, I would never have started writing children's books. Ruthie Britten could tap-dance and sing on key and was an only child, so she got private singing and private tap-dancing lessons and the lead in the sixth-grade play, and I didn't even get a speaking part. In all the world there was only one Ruthie Britten, and I got her. If I had gone to a school where she wasn't, I was certain I would have gotten the lead in the sixth-grade play, and I was certain I would have gone on to become a Broadway star. If I had gone to a school where Ruthie Britten wasn't, I would have been so busy being a famous star on Broadway, I would not have had time to write children's books.

Ruthie Britten is one reason why I write children's books. She is the only reason that has a proper name. The other reason why I write children's books is *because I can.*

I know some of the reasons why I can, and since a writer —except for authors of textbooks, diet books, and Hollywood biography or autobiography—is supposed to write about what he or she knows, and since I don't know what happened to Ruthie Britten, I shall write about why I can write for children.

When I was nine years old, my family moved from the small town of Phoenixville, Pennsylvania, to Youngstown, Ohio. Youngstown, Ohio, was a big city, big enough to be given boldface type and three complete sentences in our fourth-grade geography book.

In Phoenixville, I had just begun learning Hebrew; to me, Hebrew was God's language. The Jewish people have always relied heavily upon the word. Synagogues are solemnly free of mosaics, frescos, and other visual aids. I, like all my other classmates who were beginning to study Hebrew, made the sounds of the bold, black letters even when we didn't understand them. It wasn't necessary to understand what we were saying; God did. I memorized the important prayers in Hebrew as well as the Ten Commandments in translation. The Ten Commandments were the core of everything. They were firm and positive and absolutely without shadows, just like the big uppercase Hebrew letters. I was very pious. I was in a religious fever.

I didn't trust big cities.

Add to this black-and-white small-town world the blue laws of Pennsylvania, and you can see why I easily found sin in Youngstown, Ohio.

In Youngstown, Ohio, beer and wine were sold right in the grocery store within easy reach of pet food or cornflakes. In Pennsylvania a person had to go to a state liquor store to buy alcoholic beverages, and that was obviously more decent because Pennsylvanians kept liquor out of the hands of dog and breakfast lovers.

Also.

In Youngstown, Ohio, the movies were open on Sunday. They didn't obey the Sabbath, the Fourth Commandment: *Remember the Sabbath, to keep it holy*. They should have observed it even if they did it on the wrong day of the week.

Also.

In Youngstown, Ohio, they had a burlesque theater right on a side street of downtown.

I waited for sin to come into the classroom. I knew that it would. And I knew that Miss Mayer would bring it. I knew that, sooner or later, it would be she. Miss Mayer wore strange clothes, ones that didn't stop moving until long after she did. Furthermore, Miss Mayer had not come from Europe, she had *toured* Europe. Twice. She came to our classroom at irregular intervals to show us art. There were photographs of statues of Venus (no arms, no bra) and Apollo and other gods. There, in black and white, we could see how the pagans of Greece and Rome had made graven images. The Second Commandment clearly states: *Thou shalt have no other gods before Me. Thou shalt not make unto thee a graven image*. But, of course, long before I had moved to Youngstown, I knew that pagans not only ate too much but also didn't know enough to capitalize the word *god*.

At Christmas time, Miss Mayer came into our class and unfolded an accordion pleat of photos. When laid out flat, it showed the whole of a ceiling, the work of an Italian named Michelangelo.

I gasped.

There, in full color was Adam, absolutely stark naked with his you-know-what showing, his hand reaching out to receive the touch of life from none other than God. I knew it was God—not god, god, but God, God. The beard, the grandfather look, intense and worried. It was not a pagan god, but my very own dear God. A *graven image* of Him. There were more graven images. God creating the sun and the moon. God separating light from darkness. He was doing creation in full color just as my black-and-white word pictures had said he would.

"Where are these pictures?" I called out without raising my hand.

"In Rome. In the Vatican," Miss Mayer explained. "The Pope asked Michelangelo to paint the ceiling of this chapel called the Sistine."

"What's a chapel?"

"A place of worship, a small place, sometimes a private one."

"Is the Pope excused from the Ten Commandments?"

"Of course not," she answered. "No Christian is."

Miss Mayer then told us some facts about the artist's life. I remembered all the important ones: Michelangelo had been raised in a small town called Florence, and the Pope had called him to the big city, Rome. His early works, his small-town jobs, were statues, white marble photographed against a black ground: a David, the Virgin Mary holding her son. Only after he moved to Rome did Michelangelo dare to draw God. Only in Rome did he add color to his work.

I have now twice been to the Sistine Chapel. I have lain on my back and looked up into the face of God, high, high on the ceiling above. And even though there is no artist that I love more than Michelangelo, even though there are decades that separate that first view of the accordion-pleated reproduction from the crowds of the summertime

Sistine, even though, even though—I still see the contradiction: a graven image in a house of God.

And it is because I can look up at that active, colored ceiling and still see a black-and-white contradiction, that I can write for children. And it is because I am aware, the grown-up part of me is aware, that no child growing up today can gauge the lack of color in my own growing up, that my stuff is readable.

When my daughter, Laurie, was four years old, she was dancing around our living room, a process that involved spinning and whirling and turning, holding her arms out and ultimately stubbing her finger against the wall. The finger grew swollen and discolored, and since I was temporarily without the *off* knob on my panic button (my husband was out of town), I took her to Baptist Memorial Hospital, the hospital on our side of town, the one where she had been born.

We arrived at the X-ray room, where a young technician, Clearasil still wet on his face, adjusted the machine for us. He moved the machine this way and that, and had her move her hand this way and that. As she pointed her finger downward and upward, following his instructions, she looked up at him and said: "You probably don't remember me, but I was born here."

I am still charmed when I think of her face, the quick sucking in of her breath before reminding him of her importance, wanting him to be certain that her birth had once been the focus of hospital life.

In 1968 when I won the Newbery Award, I flew to New York a day in advance of the announcement party, and I and my two suitcases and one cosmetic case and one dress on a hanger got into the taxi that would take me from the airport to the hotel. In the way of clothing, I was prepared for anything from warm weather (it was the end of February) to Truman Capote's black-and-white masked ball or a pot party for the Panthers at Lenny Bernstein's, in case he should ask.

"Where ya from?" the driver asked.

I told him not only where I was coming from, but also (eagerly) why. Furthermore, I told him that if he read *The New York Times* the next day, he would be able to read all about me. I, of course, had visions of his telling his wife and children that he had transported this very talented lady from Newark Airport to a midtown hotel, and the kids' asking him what was I really like.

The following day, *The New York Times,* the newspaper of record, for reasons entirely within its control, chose not to print news of the Newbery and Caldecott awards that year. Between my annoyance was my embarrassment that that taxi driver would think I had lied to him.

Believing that the taxi driver would give me longer thought than it took to transport me from Newark to a midtown hotel is similar, is it not, to my daughter's belief that her birth was long remembered and well noted at Baptist Memorial Hospital?

But because I retain this ability to see myself as the center of the universe, I can write for children. And because the adult part of me can see how absolutely ridiculous I am when I am doing it, my writings are readable.

Earlier this year I was visiting a woman whose son was an art student in New York. He was home for a short vacation and had with him two sketchbooks that his mother wanted me to see. She thought that he might find a career as a children's book illustrator. His were the only truly pornographic sketchbooks that I have ever seen. He told me that most of the pictures in them came from his head, but I'm convinced that some of them were done with mirrors. I thought that they had humor and technique, but I didn't think that the children's book world was quite ready for them. Because the pictures were difficult to comment upon, I asked him what he was going to do over the summer, that is, what he was going to do *besides* the activities recorded in the sketchbook. He said he was going to be a camp counselor, and I asked him if he was looking forward to it.

"Yes," he said, "I love children."

"I don't," I said.

His mother said that she was shocked at me, Elaine, and I don't blame her. I surprised myself when I first discovered it.

"Well!" I asked her, "You don't like all housewives, do you?"

And she said no, and I said aha! and I left.

I could, of course, have asked her if she liked all adults, but I didn't. And I could have asked her if she liked all old people, but I didn't. People who profess to love all children generally think that they love all old people, too. It seems to me that people who profess to *love children* really love *childhood* and, what's more, I think, they really love only one childhood—their own—and only one aspect of it, called *innocence.*

I had asked her if she liked all housewives, people engaged with various modifications, specifications, and success in essentially the same activities. I regard childhood as a stage of life, as housewifery is. Some parts are pleasant. Some are unpleasant. Some parts are learned and stay with you all the rest of your life and, like housewifery, a lot of it is just to be got through.

I have never liked all parts of housewivery, and I've never liked all housewives. I have never liked all parts of childhood, and I've never liked all children. And I have certainly never regarded housewifery as something precious or any practitioners of its arts as beatified.

Some people make better housewives than others. Some people make better children, and it is because I don't like all children that I can write for them. But it is because the adult layer of me enables me to understand (and even sometimes have compassion for) those that I don't like, that my stuff is readable.

Several years ago I was invited to a neighbor's house for a showing of slides of a trip they had made from New Jersey to Jacksonville via various historical landmarks. (I was certain that I had been invited out of revenge. We had recently returned from a trip to Africa with 740 slides, mostly of urinating rhinos and copulating lions; we always try for action shots.)

There they were—momma and two daughters in front of the White House gate.

Click. Momma and two daughters in front of the Washington Monument. *Click.* In front of the Lincoln Memorial. *Click.* Now we were at Valley Forge. *Click.* Momma and two daughters in front of Washington's headquarters. The entire presentation was done without comment except for Momma occasionally asking the girls, "Do you remember that?" "Nuh uh." "Nuh uh." Finally, *click.* There they were at the door of Washington's headquarters at Valley Forge, and the younger of the two girls spoke up. "Oh!" she said. "Yes?" Mother responded eagerly. "Oh," the girl continued, "I remember that dress."

I thought that was a pretty dumb thing to remember after her parents had gone to all the trouble and expense to come south anti-interstates. How awful of that little girl to remember something so trivial, something as incidental as a dress.

Why, I remembered Valley Forge. It was near Phoenixville, Pennsylvania, and my parents took me there a couple of times. I remember going to Washington's headquarters and I couldn't possibly remember what I wore. What I remember is seeing the quill pen General Washington had used. *The feathered pen,* I had called it. And now, years later, I can still recall my delight in that feathered pen. I don't remember much about those trips, but I do remember George Washington's feathered pen.

The nine-year-old in me who remembers a quill pen parallels the nine-year-old who remembers only a dress. And because I still see the incidental and delight in it, I can write for children. But because I am grown and I can see the greatness of Washington as well as his feathered pen, my stuff is readable.

Not very long ago I was having a dinner party and I wanted to serve veal parmesan. I went to the supermarket and rang the buzzer that said that that was what you should do if you want special service, and I waited for the butcher to come out. When he did, I asked him if I could please have some veal cutlet, sliced thin, and he said that he didn't have any veal, but that he was expecting some tomorrow, and that I should call up to see if the veal did arrive and order then. So the following day I dialed the number of the Winn Dixie, and I got a central operator who asked me my name and my phone number and said that she would deliver my message to the butcher and call me back and tell me what he said, and that *no,* I could not talk directly to the butcher, that it was against company policy, but that she would find out about the veal and tell me, and would I please wait by my phone? I said that this was a fine state of affairs. I said, (a) I have long known that the housewife's time is less precious than that of dentists or pediatricians, and (b) I know that because I have spent some of the best years of my life waiting in those offices, but (c) I thought our country had come to a sad state, a very sad state indeed, when (d) a housewife's time is less precious than a butcher's. (You see, I don't like all housewives, but I do believe in their civil liberties.)

I served chicken to my dinner guests.

When my son Ross was eleven, we went to Montgomery Ward to purchase a gear cable for his bike. It was our second trip there; the previous trip had been fruitless. They were out of the part, but they had assured us that they would have it by the week's end. It was now three days past that, and they still did not have it in. After asking the clerk a few questions, Ross discovered that a certain model of Sears bike was the same as his Montgomery Ward one. We went to Sears. He couldn't find the part on the shelves, so he found a clerk. *She* couldn't find the part on the shelves either. She said to wait a minute, and we did, and she brought us a different clerk, who also could not find the part. The different clerk told us to go to the third floor and order it. We went to the third floor and waited in line. When our turn came, the lady asked us if this was a catalogue order, and we said we didn't know, and she asked us what we wanted and we told her, and she said that she didn't know how to do that kind of order and that she would call someone who did, and the someone-who-did came and the first thing that she asked Ross was what was the model number of his bike, and Ross said that he didn't know and that it had come from Montgomery Ward anyway, and she said that he should come back when he had the number and that they would have to do a cross-reference and that she couldn't even take his order until he had the number to tell her.

Ross turned on his heels, threw up his arms, yelled, "Dummy girl," and marched out of the store. I marched with him, proud to do so.

What I experienced at the meat counter and what my eleven-year-old son experienced at the catalogue counter was the same thing: an outsized sense of outrage. Because I have not lost my sense of outrage, because I am still furious at Ruthie Britten, I can write for children. And because I cannot yell "DUMMY GIRL," I do.

A Good
Picture Book Should...

༄

Arnold Lobel

One night a while ago, as I was watching the late news, I saw a brief bit of reportage on Dr. Seuss' seventy-fifth birthday. There was a party given for him somewhere in California. There were lots of children and balloons. Everyone looked very tanned and healthy and West Coast. The good Doctor, bearded and handsome, was there in the middle of it all. A reporter shoved a microphone up to his face.

"Don't you feel that the general quality of children's books is quite low?" asked an off-screen voice.

Dr. Seuss looked startled. He took a few backward steps.

"Now don't ask me to denigrate children's books," he said. "You're not going to make me do that." He turned away sharply and the interview was over.

I was cheered by this little exchange. Here, obviously, was a man who was not going to be made to bite the hand that had been feeding him. And I like to think that Dr. Seuss, having been around children's books for a long time, was well aware of their real worth. Perhaps he was just tired of hearing his profession endlessly bad-mouthed.

The fact is, anyone who has been involved with the field and who has followed it for a period of time can see that each year brings along a really decent portion of good stuff. Since the late thirties when Dr. Seuss began working (and before, as well), we have been bestowing an embarrassment of riches on the young readers of the world. Sure, the junk is there, mediocrity is rampant, but there is enough quality around to permit us, as a group of artists, to be proud of what we have been producing.

Proud I may be, but, in the matter of my work and of children's books in general, articulate I am not. There seems to be a loud clamor and demand for those of us who make picture books to haul our bodies up onto the podiums of America. We are asked to talk at length about what we do.

A good picture book should have a narrative that is simple. But this narrative must be composed skillfully. It must retain its interest with the repetition of many readings. Solid characterization, humor, drama, poetry . . . all these things contribute much.

A good picture book should have drawings that are neither too cartoony cute at one end of the scale, nor too sophisticated and adult at the other.

A good picture book should have artwork that is appropriate to the mood and subject matter of the story. In terms of pacing and selection of images, the artwork should be well integrated into the narrative.

A good picture book should be true. That is to say, it should rise out of the lives and passions of its creators. A book that is created as a commodity will remain just that, however successful that commodity may turn out to be.

That about completes my standard list of remarks on the subject of children's books. There is hardly enough material there to keep an audience waiting through a salad, a plate of creamed chicken on toast, and a fruit cup.

I can pad a little. I can throw in a few amusing anecdotes about the domestic life of the artist. I can divulge a bit of technical information. I can display a color separation, maybe a proof or two. I can drop some lofty names from the arts and literature of the past and present to give some tone to the sources of my inspiration. But all of this falls into the category of making a short story exceedingly long. It disguises the simple fact that the picture book speaks for itself. Its qualities or lack of them are as plain as the print on its pages.

Picture books are nice. The best ones are enormously satisfying. They are objects of pleasing self-containment, somehow capable of suggesting everything that is good about feeling well and having positive thoughts about being alive. They are filled with light and color. The paper is wonderful to the touch.

Not too many bad things happen in picture books. If they do, they usually find their way to a happy resolution at the end. I like them that way. When I feel the morbid need for unpleasantness and despair, I can read the newspaper or watch the news on television or just look out of my window. Picture books are a sanctuary from all of that.

When I am brought low by the vicissitudes of life, I stumble to my bookshelves. I take a little dose of Zemach or Shulevitz. I grab a shot of Goffstein or Marshall. I medicate myself with Steig or Sendak, and the treatment works. I always feel much better.

I often wonder how we end up doing this work, those

of us who have dedicated our lives to the making of picture books for children. We are artists, but what has pulled us away from painting large, serious canvases to hang in museums? Why are we not drawing whiskey bottles for magazine ads? As a group we seem to cling to the need for the kind of imaginative playing that childhood allows.

The cellar in the house in Schenectady where I grew up was often converted into a theater. I painted scenery on old bedsheets and put on plays for my little friends. The gratification that I obtained in producing these enterprises must have been immense for me. I have refused to bring down the curtain. The hair has turned to silver, the body sags, but my show goes on and on.

For their authors, the best books are there for a reason. Doing a book just to have something for a publisher's fall list is, of course, not the most valid of reasons. Granted, a certain amount of economic expediency can be a factor. I have, on a number of occasions, completed a book to keep the pot bubbling and the fires burning. Seldom have I been pleased with the results.

It is those books that have a subjective importance to their authors that turn out to be the good ones. When I can put myself into a frame of mind to be able to share with the reader my problems and my own sense of life's travail, then I discover that I am working in top form. It is a devious process. It involves some amount of duplicity, this transformation of adult preoccupation into stories to which children will respond.

At the moment, there is my grandmother. My parents were divorced shortly after I was born. My mother went off to work each day and I was left in the capable hands of

Grandma. It worked out fine. Grandma was strong and well organized. She had enough energy to deal with a circumstance that surely could not have seemed ideal to her.

Now Grandma has grown old. Very old. She is ninety-three and her body has become enfeebled. Her mind is gone. As I make the hour drive to the nursing home where she lives, I know that upon arrival I will not be recognized. It is a grim ordeal for me and I find that my visits to her are becoming less frequent. It is so difficult to witness life's last joke displayed with such cruelty.

I am deeply saddened by this situation. In an effort to exorcise my feelings, I have written a book. This is a book about an old person who is not feeble and who has all his faculties very much intact. I have written a book about the elderly person that I would wish my grandmother to be. That book, *Uncle Elephant,* has somehow dissipated some of my bitterness. That my character turns out to be a pachyderm has absolutely nothing to do with Grandma. I can be forgiven. I like elephants. I enjoy drawing them and I am a compulsive anthropomorphist.

I think the reader will be able to sense my emotional involvement here. If this book has weight and depth, it is because it is not arbitrary. It is an animal story for children but it has worked its way out of the fabric of my life.

For years, I've been convinced that there is an overwhelming separation between the creator of picture books and the children who read these books. This is a natural gulf caused by the age of the readers and the manner in which the books are used. Fan mail is only a partial indication of appreciation since much of it is prompted by a teacher or a librarian. But in the past months I've come to realize that the

A preparatory sketch for *Uncle Elephant.*

children are out there and anxious to indicate their responses. I need only to bolster my courage and present myself before them.

For one who is not used to large groups of children, this is not easy. Recently I've done it. I armed myself with big pads of paper and felt-tipped markers for drawing pictures. I arranged my features into a benevolent expression and sallied forth.

I found the third graders standing in the hall, waiting for me, as I entered the door of the school. They stood in several rows according to height. The tallest children in the back were holding a large banner on which was painted in big, red letters, "WELCOME MR. LOBEL." We were all nervous and we greeted each other stiffly, with the kind of formality that one associates with the meeting of diplomats at airports.

A procession was formed. We marched into the classroom. Posted on the walls of the corridor, all along the way, were many smaller signs and drawings. I saw the repetition of my name crayoned into various forms and designs. I caught glimpses of green and brown frogs and toads cut out of colored paper. I was momentarily stunned by a cartoon of my own face, small eyes, ample aquiline nose, bushy mustache. . . all accurately captured by some fledgling Daumier.

There was a special chair waiting for me. It had been wrapped in purple crepe paper. I was guided to it and was happy to sit down. The welcoming ceremony was over and I settled myself to the task of facing my public.

Miserable recluse that I am, this is not an experience that I have often allowed myself. At some point in my career, I made the decision that to create books for children was to live a life of necessary isolation. My art was to grow in an atmosphere of lonely introspection. Inspiration was not to be found in the noisy and unpredictable company of children, but in the safe, dark confines of my imagination, among the dusty pages of my book collection.

I would guess that I am correct in making this assumption. It is doubtful that my muse would be able to work for me while sitting in that third grade classroom, even in a chair of royal purple. Any ideas would be quickly obliterated by all that exuberance and enthusiasm around me. But I am becoming aware that inspiration can certainly be nourished by this kind of appreciation.

At the end of the day I staggered out of that school in a state of complete exhaustion but high with the feeling that my work was being consumed, ingested, chewed-up, and loved. The books were being *used* and I felt the need to keep on making them. After twenty years of sustained effort, I think that is called a strong second wind.

list of objectives. Indeed, history is such a sensitive subject in the school curriculum that it is constantly being manipulated to satisfy whatever image the public wishes at the moment to project. Pride in our national heritage—that is what our educators want to instill in our students, and there can be no quarrel with that. But a pride so delicate that it resists a full exposure to facts is surely not a sturdy foundation for young people, on whose commitment and imagination the future of our country depends.

Frances Fitzgerald, in her recent penetrating analysis of history textbooks *(America Revised),* has demonstrated how far we will go to keep our past palatable to all segments of our population. There are books, she points out, that are so afraid of offending Hispanic Americans that the story of the Spanish conquest of Central and South America is told with no mention of slaves, gold, or Indian massacres. The question is, how much information can you withold and not be guilty of misrepresentation? My personal experience with textbook editors bears out Ms. Fitzgerald's thesis, if only in a petty way. The changes that publishers have suggested when they reprint my books are indicative of a set of mind that is preoccupied with image rather than with truth.

I admit that it really doesn't matter what I choose to call a fictitious librarian in a book titled *George Washington's Breakfast.* I settled on the name "Miss Willing" because I am kindly disposed toward librarians. When the textbook publisher asked permission to change the name from "Miss Willing" to "Miss Schultz," I was at first baffled. Then I realized that a count must have been made of the ethnic names in the textbook and obviously "Miss Willing" contributed nothing to their ethnic score. Now, of course, I don't want to ignore any segment of our population; I applaud the trend to celebrate all strands of our culture. What I deplore is the computer mentality that pins significance to a name count. This cosmetic approach betrays a basic unwillingness to come to terms with character and issues.

Again, it is a small thing for a textbook publisher to edit the list of wedding gifts that Patrick Henry received and omit the fact that he was given six slaves. Moreover, I don't suppose it makes a vital difference if Patrick Henry's wife did not go mad (as I reveal she did) but instead simply got sick. In themselves, such omissions are of no historic moment, but I dislike the idea of anyone walking on tiptoe through our past. Don't we want to admit that our Southern leaders (and some of our Northern ones as well) owned slaves? Is it a reflection on Patrick Henry that his wife went insane? Surely a reader's imaginative grasp of Patrick Henry is challenged by the knowledge that his wife turned so violently against him and their children that she had to be confined to her room. Sick? Of course she was sick, but the habit of glossing over particulars reduces emotional context and is symptomatic, I believe, of an attempt, however well meaning, to protect children from pondering the realities of human behavior.

The study of history is about as close as children ever come in the classroom to a consideration of people, the formation of their personalities, their private and public tribulations, their conflicts, their foibles, and their strengths. This is the very *stuff* of life, yet, as every survey shows, history is not a popular subject with students. Indeed, history is often described as irrelevant. The trouble is that for political, economic, and various other indefensible reasons we are watering down history by either leaving people out of the story or by depicting them in only the simplest and most general terms. In ancient Greece, the opposite of the word for *truth* was not *falsehood* but *oblivion*. If it is not from oblivion that we need to rescue the characters of our past, it is from some place almost as indistinct.

But if on the one hand I complain that self-righteous censorship makes history too simplistic, I find on the other hand that the higher levels of academia can turn what seems to be a direct approach into a labored theory worked out in diagrams of interlocking circles and interrelated cubes. Specifically, I am thinking of a very worthy project sponsored by the National Endowment for Humanities and designed to encourage an interdisciplinary approach to American studies. In other words, following a time sequence, subject matter in language arts, in the fine arts, in social studies, and in natural science are to be studied in their relationship to each other. In actual practice this approach (whether really new or not) has been highly successful under the guidance of imaginative teachers; yet despite a unit on Heroes (concentrating on Joe Louis, Babe Ruth, and Cassius Clay), there is little indication in the descriptive literature that behind the social movements and the technological progress there were real people.

As part of an introductory explanation of the theory of this course, the following paragraph is meant to be illuminating:

"It is, in a way, like studying a can of frozen orange juice. To gain the fullest possible understanding of it, the student must come to know the can itself through inquiry into its size, shape, weight, and temperature, along with its color and the printing on it. In addition, he must understand the list of ingredients and the directions for making the juice. Then he must also open the can, make the juice, and experience its taste and consistency. Furthermore, he must taste that juice over time, since it may not always seem the same to him in all external circumstances. Only when the student has done all this, and conceivably several more steps omitted here, will he have achieved a rich, overall understanding of that entity."

It is unfair, perhaps, to take issue with a metaphor, but I can't help but ask—what about the orange? First and foremost, I want to know about the orange. Where was it grown? What was the weather like? To discuss American Studies without becoming well-acquainted with the people who write the literature, paint the paintings, sing the songs, represent the government, and advance science is like concentrating on the orange juice can, the ingredients, and the directions, without ever inquiring about the orange that once was or the tree on which it grew.

Any way you look at it, the analogy is nonsense. I am afraid I would not trust the teaching of history to a person who takes a can of orange juice so seriously. Scholarship may be the first requisite that either a teacher or writer of history should display, but surely an ability to translate the past into spirited, human terms is equally important. History sliced up into themes, sealed and packaged, makes for convenient handling and perhaps for a more comprehensive understanding, but history is not tidy. I am suspicious of scholarship that does not make a point of including the many revealing details and anecdotes that give the past its vigor. Plutarch once said that his purpose was not to write histories but lives. "Sometimes," he wrote, "an expression or a jest informs us better . . . than the most famous sieges and the bloodiest battles."

A sense of humor, it seems to me, is essential in the recounting of history. Indeed, one of the purposes in presenting the past is to develop the *watcher* in children, for the living of life and the watching of life are bound by one cord. In the long run, a sense of humor is a sense of perspective. As a writer, I hope to pass on to young people my own never-ceasing wonder at the infinitely various, amazing spectrum of human nature. It seems important to me for students to develop a sense of the irony in life. I would like them to appreciate the incredible and often bizarre twists history takes. And I want them to be exposed to those specific and unforgettable bits of information and snatches of anecdote that cling to memory like barnacles, part and parcel forever of the momentous occasions, the tragedies, the shocks that each generation suffers. Indeed, the capability of responding to the past emotionally—with tears, laughter, pain, sympathy—surely increases one's appetite for life and helps bring the landscape of human behavior into clearer focus.

We cannot afford to forget that the past is not just a series of events; it is *people* doing things. Certainly we need social frameworks to see these people in their proper contexts, but we must not limit people to their frameworks. I may not entirely agree with William Butler Yeats when he suggested that "all knowledge is biography," but I do not think the past can be either understood or assimilated until it has become alive with people. Unfortunately, there is no way to tell "the very truth" about people. Still, there is little value to any truth if one doesn't try.

Beyond the Span
of a Single Life

∾

Milton Meltzer

Sometime ago, finishing my job as judge of a literary award, I began to dispose of the books the contest had piled high in my workroom, giving them to the children of friends and neighbors. Young Alex, sitting on my floor, making his choices, was having the same lovely time I used to have with penny candy. Knowing how much he enjoys using his Kodak Instamatic, I singled out a book for his attention. "Alex," I said, "here's a good one on photography." He picked it up eagerly, took a look at its title—*Photographic History*—and dropped it instantly. "Ughhh," he groaned. "What's wrong, Alex?" I said. "H-i-s-t-o-r-y," he groaned again, as though his love, photography, had been defiled and degraded.

Young as Alex is, already he has learned to detest history. The only history he has been taught is obviously not very good history: dates and boring facts—littering the textbook, dirtying the blackboard, befouling the wall charts; and on the quizzes the unrelenting demand for the names of presidents and battles. Such fife-and-drum stuff is trivial and meaningless, yet for the child—and all too many adults —it is history. Alex saw no delight in history—only dullness.

Yet Alex, and human society, need history. Quite without realizing it, we are constantly calling upon history. Watergate was worse than the Teapot Dome scandal, we say, or what we did in Vietnam was unprecedented, or any attempt to influence Soviet Russia's treatment of dissidents will cost us détente. Alex himself will decide that his favorite football team had a better record last year than this. And his mother laments, "This school is going downhill. It was better when I went there." Historical judgments, all of them.

Try to imagine what daily life would be like if we knew no history. Without recollection, we would be adrift. For while history is not everything, it is an aspect of everything. It makes us aware of the character of our own time by helping us to see it in comparison and contrast with another. It won't tell us what to believe or how to act, it won't make us less bellicose or more peaceful, but as one scholar has put it, "it will add a new pleasure and breadth to our understanding of what it is we are. From it we can learn that we too are a part of our time, reflecting all the limitations, preconceptions, and special interests of our time." The sad truth is that "the past *is* the present. We live in that past and it does us good to know it. The present is the past, and not to experience that past imaginatively is to be dead to the real dimensions of the contemporary."

We are talking, really, about memory. An individual whose memory goes blank is in a dreadful state. It is no different for a society. A country out of touch with what happened in its past is disoriented, too. As for the child, when "it ceases to see people as static, frozen at a moment in time, but sees them instead as changing and developing creatures," we know it has taken a step toward maturity. "Such a perception," says the writer Penelope Lively, "is concerned with realizations about time and about aging, but also . . . with realizations about history. It is the perception, often startling, that places have a past, that they are now, but were also then, and that if peopled now, they were peopled then. It is a step aside from self, a step out of the child's self-preoccupation, and, therefore, a step toward maturity."

Such a step may come as often from reading as from observation. And here is where writing history for young readers comes in. It can develop their perception about the past. To have a sense of history is to have a sense of one's own humanity, and without that, we are nothing. The writer of history can help the child appreciate the past as an account of human experience, experience shaped within an historical framework. The child leads a private life, but that private life is influenced by events beyond his control. Without such awareness, the child is locked into this moment, deprived of memory, blinded.

We know how precious the recent recovery of their long-neglected or hidden past has been for black Americans, and for women. So too does the individual child need to know about the people who came before him. With the loss of oral tradition and with the fragmentation of families, books devoted to memory, both historical and personal, are terribly important to children.

In totalitarian countries, governments amputate the

collective memory. In our own country it is not force that threatens the collective memory so much as neglect. "As soon as all tradition is extinguished," Solzhenitsyn has said, "inhumanity begins." Forgetting is inhuman. Denying the child the power of memory is inhuman. The child needs to sense that this world stretches far behind him and far ahead of him, that societies change, that people evolve during their own lives, that he himself is a blend of experience and memory. He needs to know that the past as well as the present holds meaning. He needs to listen to the tales of past human suffering and hope. The young have trouble locating themselves in anything except the here and now. But they can be helped to see over the walls of their own personalities. The historian, in recollecting and patterning past actions of people and societies, sometimes makes it possible for the child to find his bearings in the bewildering currents of human diversity.

Inborn in almost all of us—but all too often extinguished by schooling—is a curiosity and a sense of wonder about the past. It is an awareness, as the historian G. M. Trevelyan put it, of "the quasi-miraculous fact that once, on this earth . . . walked other men and women, as actual as we are today, thinking their own thoughts, swayed by their own passions, but now all gone, one generation vanishing after another, gone as inevitably as we ourselves shall shortly be gone, like ghosts at cockcrow. . . ." This is the poetic side of history, the breaking down of the barriers of time and mortality so as to extend the limits of human consciousness beyond the span of a single life.

But how is history written for the young? In her carefully documented study *America Revised,* Frances Fitzgerald concluded that American history textbooks are "Towers of Babel." The texts are often carpentered by committee, homogenized by editorial teams with an eye on state adoption systems, and censored through the influence of pressure groups. Because that system encourages conformity, the texts fail to analyze basic institutions or describe the dynamics of conflict. There are honorable exceptions, but far too few of them.

As the sociologist Jules Henry once wrote, the elementary and high schools use books to educate for what he called "legitimate social stupidity." History is presented to children and adolescents in such a way as to prevent them from getting the information necessary to enable them to form an intelligent opinion about the world. "What they are permitted to learn is sifted through the fine mesh of fear and self-serving interest," he said. If you trace almost any important theme—labor, poverty, nuclear power, imperialism —through such texts, you find how superficially, evasively, nervously, fatuously, falsely they are treated.

Some of the universities, in cooperation with the U.S. Office of Education, have in the past attempted to develop materials designed to teach students how to clarify and justify their positions on public issues. Usually these projects helped students to do this by presenting dramatic case studies that focused on real persons in crucial situations. They raised sequences of challenging questions about values and facts. They mustered every device that might help the young to understand what the discussion process itself is. Perhaps the most effective way it was done was by investigation of single institutions, decisions, situations, or individuals. By zeroing in on a limited incident rather than a sweeping set of events, it was possible to go deeper, to gather more detailed information, and thereby to avoid a superficial and distorting approach. If one examines how the multinational corporation has grown, or what went into the decision to drop the atomic bomb over Japan, one might be able to draw conclusions applicable to a more general class of incidents, for questions of value persist throughout history and across cultures. The skillful teacher can make use of the parallels between human dilemmas in other times and places and today's issues in our own society.

I have no data on the current use of such experimental materials, but my impression is that it is anything but universal. Not enough teachers have been trained to use innovative approaches, not enough administrators are sympathetic to these approaches, and not enough writers are encouraged to work in this vein.

Speaking as one of the writers—that class of nonacademic professional who tries to make a living by writing trade books for young readers—I can say that after a brief ten-year period ending by the mid-1970s, most publishers lost what enthusiasm they may have had for history. The market for it simply faded away, they said. The reasons were obvious: shrinking school and library budgets, increasingly conservative school administrations, inflation of book production costs, and corporate concern for quick and immediate profits. A more subtle factor was the diminishing interest in history among the young, who have been victims, generation after generation, of badly written and unimaginative textbooks.

Only recently, a two-year, federally funded study of the effect of textbooks upon tenth-grade students of social

studies proved, once more, the dismal point. The investiga-
tors concluded that the big sums spent upon history books
were largely wasted. The majority of students either knew
most of the contents of their textbooks beforehand or gained
little after using them. One explanation offered was that
"some of the most successful textbook companies devoted
most of their efforts to packaging" rather than to content.

Surely there must be room for another kind of history
book, a better kind? In the hands of a thoughtful writer who
cares, almost any historical issue can be brought home to
young readers in a way that helps them understand its significance. Take such a basic question as the use of violence
today—the violence erupting from terrorist groups around
the globe, from Klansmen in the South, from Latin American nationalists, from authoritarian regimes stamping out
human rights. The problem of violence can be illuminated
in several different historical contexts—in the American
Revolution, in the British sailors' mutiny during the war
against France in 1798, in the labor struggles for the right to
organize in America, in the battle of young Richard Wright
to survive within the black code of his native Mississippi, in
the struggle for a Jewish homeland and the struggle for a
Palestinian homeland.

No matter what the setting, issues are often similar,
conflicts of values are often the same. The writer of such
books does not aim for consensus: the reader finishing the
book may end with many doubts remaining in his mind. But
something will have been learned about the great questions
that need to be asked, and the reader will have come to
understand that facts alone do not resolve issues. There
remain the ultimate questions of value and meaning.

My own initiation into this kind of history came nearly twenty years ago when I began work on a documentary history of black Americans. Nothing like it had been done for young readers. What came out of the impulse was the three-volume *In Their Own Words.* It drew upon letters, diaries, journals, autobiographies, speeches, resolutions, court and legislative testimony, newspaper reports, pamphlets. The black people told their story in their own words, revealing the personal experiences so neglected by the textbooks.

The words of these makers of history are rich and dramatic and moving enough. But for each documentary source the stage had to be carefully set, so I provided headnotes of historical background, helping the young reader to grasp the forces boiling up in those personal voices. And since there are gaps of silence between some voices—the words choked back, or suppressed, or lost to history—the connecting notes fling a bridge across to carry the reader within sound of another voice crying out the pain, the rage, the sorrow, the humanity.

As those volumes were appearing, Knopf's editor-in-chief conceived the plan for a new series on the American heritage to be published as the Living History Library, and asked me to write the first book, *Bread—and Roses,* dealing with the struggles of American labor in the fifty bloodiest years, 1865 to 1915. He suggested that the voices of working people speaking directly to the reader out of the past could be woven into narrative history. Usually the two approaches—the narrative account, which offers selected facts in a pattern exploring the meaning of that history as the author interprets it, and the documentary sources—are provided separately. The reader may use the one or the other, or go to both. But this editor saw that for young readers especially there was much to be gained by combining the two and spicing the dish with songs of the time and contemporary prints and photographs.

The new form turned out to be a compelling challenge. Reviewers of that first volume in the series found it "prickly with eyewitness accounts" of unionism's birth pains in the sweatshops, the factories, the railroads, and the mines. They welcomed its usefulness in supplying a new generation of readers with some illumination of the atavistic hatreds and insecurities that lay behind labor's beginnings, and saw the book as "a goad to revitalized activity in defense of industrial democracy and higher economic standards for those who remain on the outskirts of American affluence." The marriage of the two approaches, in all the books of the series, made for what one critic called "incisive and involving" treatments of the American past, "significant studies with continuing implications." When *Bread—and Roses* proved the worth of the idea, I went on to write many more books in that form, some for the same series and still more for other publishers open to what was no longer an experiment.

There are other ways to write history: no one form can possibly do. In the material with which one works, one has to find the shape that fits. Perhaps in my case I have often looked for a theme or a story that could be treated in the form I enjoy working with. In any case, whatever the form, I wish the critics would pay more attention to it. They often take the easy path of writing about the slice of history when their real function is to discuss how that history was told. The writing of history is as much an art as the writing of poetry or fiction. The writer tries to express his vision of history and to communicate it to the reader. As historian he does not invent that past, but he must give it artistic shape if he is to connect with the reader.

How to Create
a Successful Children's
Nonfiction Picture Book

❦

David Macaulay

When one is asked to contribute to a distinguished *Festschrift* (not to be confused with the leather headpiece worn by the leader of a Bavarian swing orchestra), one's natural desire is to write something appropriately distinguished. If this is not possible, then something just appropriate will probably do. I considered such topics as the influence on my graphic work of the Urbino panel, ca. 1500, but was eventually put off by the continuing dispute over who painted that delightful Rennaissance cityscape. Some believe it was Luciano da Laurana, while others insist it was Piero della Francesca. To add to the problem, a group of left-wing historians from southern California recently proclaimed the panel to be the work of Leroy Neiman. I soon realized that this confusion could only cast doubt upon my own authorship and therefore went to my second choice— a treatise on the effects of semi-nonfictional literature on the children of Wales during the first half of the late nineteenth century. It too had to be scrapped. This time because of an overwhelming paucity of research data.

It finally occurred to me that I was overreacting to the entire situation and would be better off focusing my energies on a subject that I already understand—namely the creation of children's nonfiction picture books, or C.N.F.P.B. Combining hindsight and slides, I have only recently begun to understand what it is I have apparently been trying to do for the past eight years. In addition to negligible amounts of self-knowledge, I have during this time uncovered a number of shortcuts useful in producing C.N.F.P.B. It is around these that the following paper is constructed. It is my hope that this information will not only be of interest to my colleagues but, more importantly, will encourage the up-and-coming young dabblers to consider the C.N.F.P.B. genre.

As is always the case with children's literature (C.L.), we must begin at the beginning. Let us first consider the larger question of involvement in the whole field of writing C.L.

How does one know whether or not he or she is destined to write for children? The key word here is "destined." One or onita, as the case may be, does not casually slip into the profession, but enters it with both confidence and commitment. Self-examination in the privacy of your own home holds the key to a verification of "destiny." There are a number of clues in all our lives that, upon closer inspection, clearly point the way either in or out of a C.L. career—usually.

For instance, when you are entranced by the overwhelming beauty of nature or you are running for a bus, do you see little faces on all the pansies and bluebells that dot your path? Do you imagine the neighborhood pets to be clothed in specially adapted grown-up attire? Does the front of your car appear to be smiling at you? These are but a few of the countless questions that you can ask about the seemingly irrelevant, yet the answers to which can change the course of your life and possibly the route of your bus. A positive response to even one of the questions indicates quite convincingly that you are in touch with the child inside you—the first step toward writing successfully for children and other short people.

But there are more clues that need consideration. When you spend those precious fifteen minutes with your children before they go to bed (owning one or two children, incidentally, is recommended although not required), do they beg and plead to hear the same old stories of your childhood over and over again? Do you always say yes because you feel that your childhood was perfect and you believe that children today are deprived of the wonderful experiences that made you what you are? Is your past one that simply must be shared, and are you commited to filling in the gaps of contemporary childhood? If, as you read these questions, you felt an almost uncontrollable YES erupting from deep inside you, and you are not normally troubled by indigestion, there is little doubt that you were destined to write C.L.

A similar period of introspection is now necessary to confirm your affinity for the specific area of nonfiction (N.F.). First of all, have you ever written anything resembling the following line and been unable to take it any further?

In 1906 Trevor Firthwayte-Smythe was forced to leave his home in Utah when his income, which was derived entirely from cat training, fell below the 10 percent already tithed to the church.

If the answer is yes, then chances are you were not cut out to create fiction (F.). Acknowledgment of this fact is the first step toward a career in N.F.

If you have never written anything of this magnitude, do not feel inadequate. There are a number of sure-fire nonliterary questions whose answers will quickly put to rest the doubts that may surround your calling. Can you still distinguish between television news and "Monday Night at the Movies"? Are you made noticeably uncomfortable by people who enter your home wearing masks? A yes to either of these questions bodes well for an N.F. career.

If you are still somewhat uncertain or had to answer "don't know," there is one final and ultimately revealing question that you can ask yourself. When you were a child, did your parents buy a twenty-volume set of encyclopedias and are they still receiving the accompanying annual yearbooks? A nod here ensures that your background is nothing less than ideal for a writer intent on pursuing the intricacies of N.F.

Now that you feel more secure about writing C.N.F., we can discuss the area of the picture book (P.B.). Here too there are certain standard criteria whereby you can judge for yourself your degree of visual awareness and, in turn, the appropriateness of a personal P.B. as well as a C.N.F. involvement. The most revealing question you need to ask is also the shortest. Can you spell? Tests have shown that most successfool illerstraters cannot spell well. It follows, therefore, that if you too cannot spell well, you are probably a born illerstrater. Other questions, only a little less revealing, are: Do you feel compelled to give life to inanimate objects? For instance, do you draw little legs and facial hair on pictures of fruit in the weekly supermarket supplements to your newspaper? Do you continually draw on the message pad while on the phone, and are you always approached to make the posters for your community's potluck suppers?

Think about these questions for a moment as we move from the creative to the perceptual. Are you deeply touched by pictures of children with extra large eyes? Can you relate to a smile face? Are you still amazed by carbon paper? Do you own all the books and reproductions available of Norman Rockwell's work?

If you are still not convinced of your calling, perhaps the ultimate verification of your P.B. potential lies right under your nose. Do members of your family and close friends constantly marvel at your sketches and "funny way of seeing things" and say, "You know, you should write a children's book." And in your heart, are you convinced that they are right?

If you were able to answer affirmatively any three of the preceding questions, it is more than likely that you were destined to become a C.N.F.P.B. person. From this point on, do not allow even the tiniest bit of self-doubt or introspection to block your chosen path. We are now ready to discuss the shortcuts and guidelines that I have uncovered in my own work and am delighted to share at this time with my worthy readers.

Before you can even begin to create a C.N.F.P.B., you must determine for which age group your work will be slanted. There are those in the field who believe there is no fundamental difference between creating a C.N.F.P.B. and an A.N.F.P.B. (adult nonfiction picture book). This is nonsense! The popularity of this misguided attitude has, over the past few years, been primarily responsible for the production of a number of troublesome books. It must be crystal clear to librarians and booksellers alike what age reader you are aiming at. A firm commitment to age categorization on your part will ensure that your book is placed on a shelf of appropriate height and in the correct department.

Fortunately there are only two age categories. They are 0 to 10 and 11 and over. It might be helpful to jot them down on a piece of paper that can then be fastened to the wall over your work area.

The best way to determine the optimum age category for your work is to take some samples of it to your next cocktail party. If they get no reaction or provoke only rude remarks, then obviously yours is the 0 to 10 group. It is books for this group that the contents of this paper are intended to encourage. You may think it more appropriate to pass the samples around among children, but this, in my opinion, leads only to confusion. Most children, after all, have never even thought about childhood. I have always found it much more meaningful to go to those who have children or who were once children themselves for comments. They, after all, are much more likely to have their attitudes toward childhood in perspective.

Next we must discuss the content of a C.N.F.P.B. In selecting appropriate subject matter, it is always a good rule to underestimate rather than overestimate a child's intelligence. Keep the subject matter simple and, whenever possible, write about things they already know. Writers often set out, quite mistakenly, to "broaden horizons" and "spark imaginations." Stay away from articles and reviews in educational magazines that harbor and promote these misguided ideals. The primary function of a C.N.F.P.B. is to increase a child's sense of security. This can be accomplished most effectively by telling them what they already know or showing them how to make things they already know how to make. Just imagine how the self-confidence of children will grow when they see in a book that they are thinking and doing exactly what they are supposed to be thinking and doing at their age.

Above all, the writer should not let his or her own interests interfere with or influence the choice of subject matter. For example, if you are interested in architecture, don't fall into the trap of thinking that anyone else is. This might sound rather elementary, but it does happen. It is particularly important not to confuse children with descriptions of entire buildings or their history. Instead, children should be encouraged to build forts and clubhouses or to hide under porches and inside large bushes. This is the kind of information they need and can deal with best. Don't burden them with concepts, or attempt to explain why things are the way they are. First of all, they don't care, and secondly, you might get it wrong.

When a subject becomes too complicated, you run the risk of crossing over into the other age category. This results in having everyone from the 11 and over group crowding into the children's areas of libraries and bookstores, blocking all the light intended for your young readers, not to mention risking the danger of an entire family's gathering around a single child trying to read his or her C.N.F.P.B. Think for a second of the effect this could have on the child!

Age category crossover (A.C.C.O.) can be avoided by

remembering only two words when creating a C.N.F.P.B. They are *simplistic* and *predictable*. Subjects that I consider highly appropriate for our age group include: how a steam locomotive works; thirty-five ways to make a clubhouse using only one blanket and two chairs; how to transport mud into a house; and books on getting lost.

I should also warn you that at no time during the planning of a C.N.F.P.B. should you consider the book as a whole. Obviously it should contain some words and some pictures, but don't try weaving the two together. It is impossible to predict which of the two the individual child will want. Some children are word oriented while others are picture oriented. If you successfully integrate the words and pictures and produce what is often called a "unified" C.N.F.P.B., you run the risk of converting a child of one preference to the other, perhaps less comfortable, form. The whole problem can easily be avoided by simply making up the words first and then fitting the pictures around them somehow or vice versa. Make an effort at all times to separate words and pictures that would seem to belong together. If a piece of text describes or perhaps clarifies a particular picture, insert it in the book as far away as possible from that picture.

When you're producing the text for a C.N.F.P.B., a couple of fairly obvious rules should be noted. First, avoid lucid text. Forcing children to move quickly and effortlessly over a passage denies the interaction with each word that is required to develop their spelling skills. Second, you should always attempt to write down to your audience. If you can put silly endings on some of the big words (no more than two syllables), you will more than likely win the affection of your young readers. Here is an example of text that has not been successfully written down:

> The people of Chutreaux had constructed the
> longest, widest, highest, and most beautiful cathedral
> in all of France.

The preferred written-down version reads as follows:

> All the teeny, tiny little people had made the very,
> very biggest church in all of Francy-wancy.

Although the comparison clearly speaks for itself, let me just add that successful writing down will further reduce the possibility of undesirable A.C.C.O.

Before we move on to the picture-making part of our discussion, I think it would be appropriate to bring up one of the most serious issues in all of C.N.F.P.B.-making, and that is the inclusion of humor. Let me just say that no C.N.F.P.B. should under any circumstances contain humor. If we make the mistake of encouraging children to laugh at nonfiction, what is to stop them from laughing at all sorts of other important things? We do a tremendous disservice to children by encouraging them, even unintentionally, to believe that life is funny. Humor can only confuse a child's still cloudy perception of the difference between nonfiction and reality.

Pictures for a C.N.F.P.B. are by definition always done in full color, and the reasons for this are obvious. Remember that a child can be swayed by the use of color even if you haven't been able to resolve completely the content part of the book. Research has shown that children will often thumb through a book containing black-and-white illustrations before deciding on whether or not to buy it. If the book is in color, they are much more likely to pick it up and have it paid for before they realize what's inside it.

The economic realities of our world make it more and more difficult to produce full-color books. However, there are some reasonable alternatives. You should at least design the covers for your books using as many colors as possible. If the pictures inside are all black and white, you should encourage the production people to spill minute amounts of glue around the edges of the pages when the book is being bound. This will make it extremely difficult for a child to open the book in the shop, since most of them usually do not carry a small knife or other sharp instrument. This production technique, combined with a full-color cover, will make your book almost as successful in sales as a full-color book.

In discussing the artwork for a C.N.F.P.B., one need only recall those two words—*simplistic* and *predictable.* If you have a natural ability to draw in convincing perspective, you will have to work a little harder at trying to make your pictures look flat. Many problems can be eliminated by simply avoiding certain common pitfalls. For instance, do not draw railroad tracks. If you absolutely must, then be sure to make them look as much like a ladder as possible. Never include the same object in different sizes in the same drawing. This will almost always create the troublesome illusion of space. If, when you have finished a picture, there is more of the page left over than you thought there would be, fill it in with lots of little things. Children love little things. I have found that bricks are particularly useful in this situation, but virtually any complex texture will do the trick, including concentric shapes and little animals locked together.

I would like to conclude with a caution that may, at first glance, seem obvious: A good C.N.F.P.B. author must not in either word or picture give information that will be useful to the reader in another context. Try to ensure that once the reading is completed and the book has been closed, there will be no lingering traces.

Any clues in a picture, for instance, that might increase a child's awareness of and sensitivity toward his or her environment should be completely removed. Be vigilant in your editing, for it is essential that we not get tangled up with the reader's imagination. Plan and create your books so that even if a little information should rub off on the reader, you have not "reached" them in any significant way. "Reaching" is not your responsibility.

I trust and believe that careful reading and studying of these clues and insights will prepare almost anyone for a career in the C.N.F.P.B. world. In fact, you will probably be surprised at how easy it is, with this discussion under your belt, to create books that are virtually indistinguishable from many of those being created by professionals in the field. The satisfaction of knowing that your work will fit in so perfectly with so much of what has been and is still being produced is not only heartwarming but is also a genuine sign of personal success. Remember those two words—*simplistic* and *predictable*—and welcome to C.N.F.P.B., one of life's most rewarding career path alternatives (C.P.A.).

Science Done Here

∾

Laurence Pringle

The nineteenth-century philosopher Søren Kierkegaard told of a man who saw a sign in a shop window: "Philosophy Done Here." He rushed into the shop to buy some, only to be told that the sign itself was for sale.

The subject here is science books, and Kierkegaard's story can easily be adapted to the late twentieth century: change the words to "Science Done Here" and put them on a T-shirt. This essay explores what it means to "do science," why an understanding of science is especially important now, and how children's books can help.

Perhaps it is best to start with a list of what "doing science" is *not*. It is not doing technology, which is one way of applying knowledge gained from science. Automobiles, antibiotics, calculators, pesticides, and nuclear-powered electric generating plants are technological feats that depend, to varying degrees, on knowledge gained from science. The knowledge did not have to be used that way, but for cultural, economic, and political reasons it was. Technology and science are inexorably linked, but it is important to remember that they are entirely different enterprises with different goals.

Doing science is also not following some mythical "scientific method." This term refers to a way to design and carry out an experiment, or at least how to describe the experiment for publication. Most scientists admit that their attempts to solve a problem often bear little resemblance to the scientific method. Besides, doing science involves not just experimentation but also observation, measurement, and logic. Each is used to varying degrees in different fields; each is appropriate to certain kinds of inquiries.

Soon after a wildlife biologist published an account of his wolf studies, he received a letter from a science teacher who chastised him for the lack of a "control" group of wolves in his "experiment." But there was no feasible way *experimentally* to answer the questions he had about wild wolves. He was doing science by logical deductions from careful observations.

Doing science is also not memorizing a lot of names and numbers. Measurement yields numbers, but the numbers are just a useful crutch for the human mind. They help us understand reality, but they are not reality. Many children go through a stage of fascination with numbers, world records, batting averages, and the like. And when we begin to learn about plants or birds or dinosaurs, naming them is usually step one. It is satisfying to recognize poison ivy or a red-tailed hawk or *Tyrannosaurus.* But naming or measuring something is not knowing it. The numbers and names answer "what" questions, rather than the more complex and intriguing "how" and "why" questions.

Doing science means being curious, asking questions. It means having a healthy skepticism toward authority and announced truths. It is both a way of looking at the world and a way of thinking. It values both fantasy and reality, and provides a framework for telling the difference.

Economist Kenneth Boulding has written that "science is the product of organized fantasy about the real world." Obviously, professional scientists have a great deal of specialized training and knowledge, but what they do, at its simplest, can be and is practiced by ordinary people. Scientists just apply plain, everyday ways of thinking to questions or problems that most people don't think about seriously or carefully.

To do science is to acknowledge that the world is a complex place but that the complexity can be explored and understood, and that there is order and unity in its diversity. At its core, science is a hopeful activity. Psychiatrist Karen Horney believed that young children are naturally joyful, unafraid, warm, and spontaneous. To this I think we can add curious and hopeful. Since science at its best stands for hope, curiosity, truthfulness, and the joy of discovery, you might suppose that children would clamor for more science in their lives. This is not the case. According to a study conducted in the late 1970s, at the end of elementary school just 25 percent of boys and only 3 percent of girls say they would consider a science career. National test scores in both biological and physical sciences have declined significantly.

Science teaching is scarce in elementary and middle schools, and many science programs reinforce the notion that doing science means memorizing facts, jargon, and numbers that seem irrelevant to everyday life. Scientists themselves have contributed to illusions about how they work and what the results mean. As a result, the public feels that science is much too complex for ordinary folks, and that it is a source of final, absolute answers rather than a continual search for truth.

This massive misunderstanding of science is taking its toll. Although there is no lack of scientists, women and ethnic minorities are poorly represented. Ill-prepared to tell facts from fantasies and wishful thinking, people support a thriving UFO industry, astrology industry, and other pseudoscience enterprises with millions of dollars annually. By itself, this may be harmless, but irrationality spills over into other areas. Science illiteracy has other, greater costs.

We live in an age when decisions involving science and technology can have enormous effects on everyone. Scientific knowledge—or a lack of it—plays a vital part in food-growing, health, and energy matters, for example. Decisions about such matters affect the quality of our lives, and perhaps the lives of many generations to come. Already there have been instances in which reasonable, sound health measures were subverted because of science illiteracy among Congressmen, journalists, and the public. We are paying for our ignorance.

Books reflect our culture, so it is not surprising to find some children's books that could only thrive amidst science illiteracy. In a recent children's book about astrology, for example, nearly all of the text was neutral or mildly positive in tone. Readers were even given detailed instructions for preparing a horoscope. Only in the last few pages was the validity of astrology questioned seriously. Finally, in the last line, it was dismissed as nonsensical magic. This attempt to have it both ways—to appeal to ignorance, then belatedly appeal to reason—was disrespectful to readers of any age, and especially so to children.

Another author wrote of "unexplained happenings" and "unsolved mysteries," such as an alleged kidnapping carried out by robots aboard a flying saucer. "Experts don't know the answers" was the claim, though expert and prosaic explanations are available, had the author or publisher sought them. Given incomplete, distorted information, readers were encouraged to draw their own conclusions about the so-called mysteries. This sort of book exploits and fosters science illiteracy; it also shows that authors and editors can be science illiterates.

Commercial exploitation of ignorance is never pretty, but books like these, fortunately, are only a small fraction of those published. Furthermore, the overall quality of children's science books has improved in the past decade or two. The "gee whiz" approach to scientific and technological developments is vanishing. People are more conscious of interconnections. They have learned to expect side effects—which someone called "wormholes in the fruits of technology"—so that few books now read like press releases from industry or government. There are also fewer books about animals as isolates; the interdependence of living things and their environment is acknowledged and celebrated.

There have also been some encouraging changes in other media. For decades, commercial television has abounded with pseudoscience of the worst sort. The few programs dealing with real science tended to emphasize colorful, charming subjects. Michael Arlen, television critic for *The New Yorker,* wrote, "It wouldn't kill us to know a little bit about the so-called boring stuff, and it might in fact kill us *not* to know about it."

The public television series "Cosmos," first shown in 1980, may have helped viewers begin to distinguish between some truths and some illusions about themselves and the universe. Astronomer Carl Sagan, host of the series, said, "I would be very pleased if viewers left the entire series without remembering a single fact—provided they found rekindled some of that ancient human joy in understanding the natural world, in the celebration of nature."

Aiming at eight- to twelve-year-olds, Children's Television Workshop produced "3-2-1 Contact" with a goal of showing "science as rational, but also intuitive, neat, but also messy, and characterized not only by patience and rigor, but by wit and playfulness as well."

These goals have been met by the finest children's science books down through the years. Whether the subject is the moon or a mouse, you can find a core of integrity in these books. Both subject and reader are treated with respect.

Scientists are portrayed as humans. They sometimes make mistakes, and compete or squabble among themselves. Their curiosity leads them to ask questions much like the ones other people ask. What they learn may or may not stand the test of time or the scrutiny of other minds. It will certainly lead to more questions.

There is, of course, some jargon in most of these books. An irreducible minimum of terms is vital in order to tell a story or explain an idea. Authors who are obsessed with naming things, who feel that a sort of crossword-puzzle knowledge is wisdom, usually aim for maximum jargon. But a minimum of terms and their definitions helps clear the reader's path from idea to idea, and it is the ideas that really matter.

As a writer, I felt the burden of scientific terms and their definitions most acutely in my book *Death Is Natural.* The main ideas of the first chapter were that death is inevitable and necessary, and that minerals and other matter making up living things are continually recycled on earth. The chapter's "character"—a rabbit—died on the first page, but there was still a story to tell. What happens to a dead animal? Where does it *go?*

Just as readers may feel an urgency to find out, I wanted to get on with the story. Before long, however, there was that irreducible minimum of terms (element, atom, molecule) to explain. I felt impatient with those paragraphs, and suppose that readers do too. That I chose *not* to use a dozen other terms having to do with decay is some consolation.

At a recent conference on children's books, an editor declared that accuracy is the single most important characteristic of science books. Well, sure, accuracy ranks right up there with apple pie, but I wonder, "accuracy of what?" Minor details, major ideas, values, attitudes? Which would you rather read: a book marred by some factual errors that is also sprightly, inspiring, and memorable, or one that is perfect in every factual detail but dull as a hoe? We should not have to make such a choice, since most publishers routinely pay experts to check manuscripts of nonfiction books. (Of course, experts can be careless, make or miss mistakes, and also may disagree among themselves.) The perfect book has yet to be published, but the best science books are accurate in details and especially in concepts. Respect for the truth, to the extent it is known, is part of the appealing integrity of doing science.

A special problem of children's science books is their brevity. Writers cannot afford to dawdle or be encyclopedic. They must first have a firm grasp of the overall subject, then select and convey the key ideas. Done well, this produces a highly accessible introduction to a subject—just right for adults, it is often remarked.

In some fields of science the knowledge is more secure than in others. Whatever the subject, however, the reader should not be given the idea that everything is known, and that he or she just absorbed it all in sixty-four pages. Almost invariably it is safe to say that there's more to learn, and more to discover.

Senator Daniel Moynihan of New York once wrote, "A century ago the Swiss historian Jacob Burckhardt foresaw that ours would be the age of 'the great simplifiers' and that the essence of tyranny was the denial of complexity. He was right. This is the single greatest temptation of the time. It is the great corrupter, and must be resisted with purpose and with energy."

Thus it is quite appropriate and respectful in certain children's science books to say, "This stuff is complex and the whole story isn't here; in fact, we humans are having a hard time dealing with the complexity."

The doing of science depends on such special human qualities as curiosity, passion, creativity, and veracity. Partly because of these characteristics, science has been called the greatest hope of the human race. Children's books have a vital role to play. They can make science and the universe more accessible to young people. They can stand for and appeal to the finest characteristics and highest aspirations of the human species.

Criticizing the Critics

∽

Millicent Selsam

In 1963 George Sarton, historian of science, wrote a delightful article on the foibles of reviewers of "learned" books. Because so much of what he had to say then is valid today regarding the reviewing of science books, I will repeat some of his best jibes at reviewers of different types.

First, he said, there is "James the Egotist," who does not think half as much of the books entrusted to him, or of the author, as he does of himself. His purpose is to show off his own superior qualities much more than it is to explain the book he is reviewing.

Then there is "John the Obscure," who tries to hide ignorance and meanness under a veil of spurious profundity. His statements are ambiguous. They suggest, insinuate, and leave the reader not knowing what to think of the book.

The "impartial" critic leaves us in the lurch. Apparently afraid of writing a real opinion, he says both yes and no to the book in the same paragraph. This type of critic sometimes finds it easier to copy the jacket blurb.

"Pliny the Elder" indulges in superlatives. A book is either all bad or all good—and there is nothing in between.

The "pedantic" critic sees nothing but the faults and makes capital of them. This type concentrates on errors (often trivial), so much so that the casual reader might be led to believe the entire book is untrustworthy.

Every author who has a number of science books to his or her credit must surely recognize from personal experience some of these reviewer types. But what, then, is a good review?

The first objective of a review should be to give the reader a good idea of what the book is about. Many reviewers just launch into an attack against what they perceive as faults, without describing the book's content first. A cantankerous reviewer can say something like this: "If the bird pictured on page 23 is a nuthatch, it has the wrong arrangement of feet." The author, on reading this, hurries to look at page 23 and finds that all he or she wanted there was a *bird* and it did not matter what kind of bird or how its feet were arranged. But this reviewer was overcome by the urge to tell the world what he knew about bird feet, complete with scientific names (Anisodactyle for the three plus one arrangement and Zygodactyle for the two plus two arrangement). Appropriate enough for reviewing a technical book for scientists, but altogether out of place when commenting on a book meant for children from six to eight years of age. Reviewers of science books should look for accuracy, but they should also keep in mind that "one mistake does not a bad book make." I love the following sentence I found in a recent review: "I could list a few errors, but they are so trivial that I would be ashamed to do so."

The second consideration is the age level for which the book is written. I have had experience with reviewers who criticized a book because it did not give exceptions to a general rule. For instance, amphibians lay their eggs in water, but there is a salamander or two that does not. It is hardly a fair criticism of a book about amphibians in general if it doesn't go into the habits of the rare exception. In science there are few statements you can make to which you cannot find an exception. A young reader must first learn what is generally true before dealing with the exceptions. A good reviewer is keenly aware that a science book for children should start from the background and experience of children. The book must be simple and clear and enable the reader to understand, without vulgarizing or talking down or diluting the subject. The reviewer should appreciate that the author has to stop before the attention of the young reader is lost. The author cannot mention everything that is known on a subject.

A third characteristic of a good review is that it will give the reader a sense of how the book fits in and/or compares with other literature on the subject. However, when two books are compared, an effort should be made to distinguish what each of the authors was trying to do. One book may have been intended to offer standard information on turtles and another may be taking a look at predation in the animal world, using turtles as an example. Can the latter book be properly faulted because it does not include all the standard information on turtles? Or, suppose the reviewer is giving his or her opinion on two shark books. One tells the life history of sharks. The other tells how scientists distinguish one kind of shark from another. Is it fair, in comparison, to call the classification book of limited scope when the author had an entirely different goal—to teach the classification of sharks? The reviewer should give the author his or her due and recognize what he or she set out to do—not what the reviewer imagines the book should have been.

I recently read a review of a book about wildlife on the African grasslands. The book described the habits and habitats of lions, leopards, cheetahs, and zebras, and their interaction around a waterhole. The reviewer said, "There is inordinate attention paid to the feeding habits of carnivores, such as the lion, hyena, cheetah, and other scavengers. It would have been preferable to focus on the beauty of the African grasslands and the animals, rather than the destruction occurring in the web of life." Here is a clear case of a reviewer who did not properly judge the book that was written because the reviewer *wished* for an entirely different book.

In order to be a good critic of science books, a reviewer must have an understanding of what a good science book is. I feel very strongly that science books must not only give facts, but show how these facts are related in the broad concepts of science. For a great many years, in the field of biology, men classified plants and animals and gave names to thousands of species. But these names and classifications were just a lot of interesting facts until Charles Darwin gave them *meaning.* Living things that looked more alike than others were in the same group because they were *related* to one another through descent from common ancestors. In other words, they had evolved from similar forms of life. Today we know that the concept of evolution changed the whole history of biology because Darwin had found general rules that explained a lot of facts.

A good review should point out incorrect concepts such

as teleology and anthropomorphism. Teleology explains everything in science in terms of purpose. For example, you may find a sentence that says, "Birds fly south *so that* they will have food and warmth for the winter." This is an oversimplification and explains nothing. A scientific explanation of why birds fly south would say that scientists are still trying to find out what triggers bird migration. It is a complicated matter involving hormones, day length, etc. A well-thought-out explanation would describe what the best theories are and what areas are still to be explored.

Anthropomorphism, another incorrect concept, treats animals as though they had human characteristics. Does an earthworm make up its *mind* that it cannot escape from a jar? How can it, when it has no mind to make up? There are still too many so-called science books that misrepresent the nature of animal behavior. Errors such as teleology and anthropomorphism should be pointed out in reviews.

Good questions to ask are: Does the book lead to an appreciation of the method of science? Does it encourage observation? Does it merely describe experiments or does it make a young person aware of the nature of an experiment and the need for controls in order to draw valid conclusions? Good science books can help develop intelligent scientific attitudes that would make children skeptical of nutrition fads, diet claims, and gurus. They can make young people less susceptible to the idea that mysterious unknown forces control our lives and more aware of the role science plays in our society.

The application of scientific knowledge has made tremendous contributions to our everyday life. It has given us information about diet, vitamins, microbes, antibiotics, food processing, and other technical developments that we take for granted. Good science books can help young people to see that science must be enriched by human values and ideals. The intelligently informed young person can be an active citizen about scientific matters such as H bombs, nuclear power, and germ warfare, instead of standing by bewildered by what it is all about.

A reviewer should look for qualities in a book that will stimulate the young reader to seek further information on its subject. The other day I was standing before a children's book display at the American Museum of Natural History. A young woman and her son were looking at a book of mine called *Greg's Microscope.* She did not know that I was the author of the book, but she turned to me and said, "I'm afraid to buy this book because I might have to buy him a microscope." I said, "That would be wonderful." And I did mean it would be wonderful if the book inspired the boy to want his own microscope.

A good book on the microscope should make a young person want a microscope. A good book on trees should help a young person see not only a tree, but its special leaves, flowers, and its different bark, branches, and buds. It should make a walk through the woods ten times more interesting than it was before he or she read that book on trees.

"James the Egotist," "John the Obscure," and "Pliny the Elder" will probably always be with us as reviewers. The good reviewer, however, using sound criteria for judging science books for children, has an important and challenging contribution to make to science, children, and books.

Nonsense Verse: The Complete Escape

∾

Myra Cohn Livingston

They went to sea in a sieve, they did;
  In a sieve they went to sea:
In spite of all their friends could say,
On a winter's morn, on a stormy day,
  In a sieve they went to sea.
And when the sieve turned round and round,
And every one called, "You'll all be drowned!"
They called aloud, "Our sieve ain't big;
But we don't care a button, we don't care a fig;
  In a sieve we'll go to sea!"
      Far and few, far and few
        Are the lands where the Jumblies live:
        Their heads are green, and their hands are blue;
        And they went to sea in a sieve.[1]

It is heartening for those of us with feet of clay to know
that there is a world where Jumblies may sail off in a sieve.
Here a cow may jump over the moon and oysters wear shoes
as they scramble to shore. This other realm, lawless and

foolish, offers refuge from reason. It remains something of a paradox that we humans, who pride ourselves on behaving as thinking, sensible beings, should be so eager to escape to a place of chaos, violence, and sometimes death. Yet we do so willingly. It is even more remarkable that we enter and exist with laughter—even hilarity!

Nonsense is a literary genre whose purpose it is to rebel against not only reason but the physical laws of nature. It rejects established tenets, institutions, pokes fun at rational behavior, and touts destruction. It champions aberrations. This, at first glance, would seem to set the stage for tragedy. Our emotions would normally send up a warning signal that such rebellion is bound to end in anarchy. And so it would be if this defiance of reason were taking place in our everyday world.

But the masters of nonsense verse create another world. Here objects of reality are recognizable but put to inane purposes; absurd people and situations abound, and incongruities are juxtaposed in a fixed manner.

Although nonsense, like poetry, eludes definition, it seems important to me at a time when so much verse is being written in the name of nonsense that we seek to establish those elements that are the province of nonsense, and those that simply fall into the categories of humor, wit, word-play, parody, and wild imagination or illusion. Most critics would agree with G.K. Chesterton that nonsense is "lawless and innocent";[2] they would accept Phyllis Greenacre's contention that it is "not only the lack of reason or expected order, but it is the defiance of reason which men value most,"[3] and agree with Vivian Noakes that it "is a game played by a rational, methodical mind."[4]

But it is necessary, I believe, to go further and spell out the conditions under which we find the best in nonsense. Those who write nonsense verse must use the touchstones of reality—physical laws as well as objects and people— and transfer them, through carefully controlled imagination, to an *impossible* world, a world that poses no threat to us. It is essential that these conditions be carried out in order that we feel no sympathy, empathy, or compassion. The genius of the writer of true nonsense is such that we are able to enter his world with no physical or emotional threat to ourselves. Nonsense verse does not mirror back the frailties or weaknesses of humankind. Rather does it enable us, as well as those who inhabit its realm, to effect a complete escape.

In order to make this escape, in order to arouse laughter, nonsense verse relies on a number of elements, in various combinations, to create its impossible world. It uses humor, but only that which deals with impossible human aberrations:

> I eat my peas with honey.
> I've done it all my life.
> It makes the peas taste funny
> But it keeps them on the knife.

This anonymous verse presents a humorous idea, out of the bounds of proper manners and expected taste sensations, to be sure, but it is not impossible—the thing can be done. John Ciardi's "Mummy Slept Late and Daddy Fixed Breakfast" and Kaye Starbird's "Eat-It-All-Elaine" are typical of this sort of fun. It is unlikely that a child would use a hacksaw or torch to cut a waffle, or that Elaine would consume Kleenex, birch bark, prune pits, and a stinkbug—but it *is* possible. None of this is nonsense as we find it in N.M. Bodecker's "Poundcake from Ealing":

> Poundcake from Ealing
> and tea from Darjeeling
> keeps young pigs from squealing
> while tea
> from other locations
> restores the sensations
> in wilted carnations
> —when taken with jam from Dundee.[5]

This clearly nonsensical poem is in the tradition of Edward Lear, whose limerick characters are offered a variety of foods to effect cures, most ludicrous of which is butter offered to the Old Man of Prague that rids him of the plague!

Closely related to humor is wit, which depends on a writer's cleverness, lively comparisons, and/or quick repartee. Richard Wilbur's *Opposites* are unusually fine wit, but not nonsense:

> The opposite of *doughnut?* Wait
> A minute while I meditate.
> This isn't easy. Ah, I've found it!
> *A cookie with a hole around it.*[6]

Limericks abound with wit, but are often mistaken for nonsense:

> There once was a pious young priest
> Who lived almost wholly on yeast;
> "For," said he, "it is plain
> We must all rise again
> And I wish to get started, at least."

Our understanding of yeast as a leavening property is used here in a spirited comparison; but this is merely foolishness, not nonsense. Wit and cleverness can, however, be used as part of nonsense, and are easily detected in Lewis Carroll's parodies that run through the whole of the *Alice* books:

> "You are old, Father William," the young man said,
> "And your hair has become very white;
> And yet you incessantly stand on your head—
> Do you think, at your age, it is right?"[7]

Carroll's wit justifiably turns the sacrosanct Father William of Robert Southey's "The Old Man's Comforts and How He Gained Them" into one person whose actions are clearly nonsensical. The same pattern is repeated in "The Aged, Aged Man" where Wordsworth and the leech-gatherer of "Resolution and Independence" become one and the same. Carroll goes beyond parody, however, by adding sheer impossibilities; one cannot "dig for buttered rolls" or boil the Menai bridge in wine!

William Jay Smith in *Mr. Smith & Other Nonsense* has given us some good nonsense, but his imitations of Lear in "The Floor and the Ceiling" and "The Antimacassar and the Ottoman" clearly point out how difficult it is to achieve true nonsense. In the first, both Floor and Ceiling are happy together; they buy each other gifts, dine, and sing. After a spat, however, the Ceiling flies out the door, leaving the Floor alone and the house in ruins. In the second, the Antimacassar and the Ottoman both express a desire to fly to Turkistan, leaving behind a room they abhor hung with "arsenic green" drapes, and decorated with an "ugly painted scene of Venice," an artificial fire, and cold linoleum among other unattractive trappings. Yet, since the Ottoman "cannot fly" and the Antimacassar is "pinned in permanence to a chair," they remain in the room and do not leave.[8]

Wit and humor are both used. Personification parallels that of Lear, whose pairs such as the Nutcracker and the Sugar Tongs, the Table and the Chair, the Duck and the Kangaroo also wish to effect departure. Nonsense, as Lear saw it, offered adventure, escape, and happiness through an abiding belief in the power of imagination. All of Lear's characters were aware of their limitations, yet attempted the impossible. It is in the nature of nonsense that the impossible be accomplished, that the bounds of reality be broken. Smith well understood this up to the point where he failed to make the final leap and *free* the Floor, the Antimacassar, and Ottoman from reality. We feel compassion with the Floor left in a pile of rubble and empathy for those who cannot escape from ugliness. It is the same sort of sympathy we feel when Edward Lear, himself, broke down in "The Courtship of the Yonghy-Bonghy-Bò."

> From the Coast of Coromandel
> Did that Lady never go;
> On that heap of stones she mourns
> For the Yonghy-Bonghy-Bò . . .[9]

When Lear allowed his emotions to enter, the spell of the nonsense world vanishes. When we begin to identify, as readers and listeners, we have made no escape. We are back in reality.

Although some aspects of the worlds of fantasy and surrealism may be used as part of nonsense verse, they do not, strictly speaking, meet the standards of the nonsense world. The land of fantasy may not be real, but it is governed by its own laws and those who people it are bound by these laws, as well as those who enter it. Fantasy and surrealism mirror our emotions. Nonsense dare not do so.

Those who write nonsense verse have many tools. Inversions, what Kornei Chukovsky calls "topsy-turvies" and Peter and Iona Opie call "Tangletalk," are staples of nonsense verse. Oral rhymes abound with inversions:

> One dark day in the middle of the night
> Two dead boys got up to fight . . .

Inversions constitute the body of this anonymous verse:

> 'Tis midnight and the setting sun
> Is slowly rising in the west.
> The rapid rivers slowly run.
> The frog is on his downy nest.
> The pensive goat and sportive cow,
> Hilarious, leap from bough to bough.

This is not nonsense, but rather a self-contained (albeit inverted) world dependent upon our recognition of certain physical laws. Inversions, used one after the other, do not constitute nonsense poetry, because a system has been set up, rather like a code, that we have only to unravel to understand. The world of true nonsense must admit reality and then proceed to distort it.

Another sort of inversion is found in some nursery rhymes:

> I saw a peacock with a fiery tail
> I saw a blazing comet drop down hail
> I saw a cloud with ivy circled round
> I saw a sturdy oak creep on the ground
> I saw . . .

Here the insertion of commas (after comet, cloud, and oak) will make perfect sense of what at first sight appears to be nonsense.

Inversions, in the hands of a fine nonsense poet, are used judiciously. The beginning of Carroll's "The Walrus and the Carpenter" is a good example:

> The sun was shining on the sea,
>   Shining with all his might:
> He did his very best to make
>   The billows smooth and bright—
> And this was odd, because it was
>   The middle of the night.[10]

Neulogisms are certainly necessary to some nonsense. Dennis Lee's Crankabeast or Psychapoo, Shel Silverstein's Yipiyuk carry faint recognition of things with which we are familiar. Jack Prelutsky's Snopp, Lurpp, and Grobbles are similarly loaded with clues, as are Laura Richards' Bobbily Boo and Wollypotump, although much in Richards strikes me as derisive. Often we encounter phonetic spellings, particularly for the sake of end rhyme in limericks. Phonetic reading will decode the seeming mystery of David McCord's beginning lines for "Pome":

> Hlo
> Outen myuncles varmule see
> a nash a noak anna napple tree . . .[11]

Certainly, with an ever increasing interest in Lewis Carroll, we become more familiar with portmanteau words such as *frabjous* or *frumious.* The first stanza of "Jabberwocky" is indeed as close to pure nonsense as we can come. But the meanings of the words can be learned from Humpty-Dumpty and Carroll's own notations. The element of nonsense is not only in the passage as we read it, but heightened in the explanation:

> 'Twas brillig, and the slithy toves
> Did gyre and gimble in the wabe:
> All mimsy were the borogoves,
> And the mome raths outgrabe.[12]

Hence, the literal English of the passage is:

> It was evening, and the smooth active badgers were scratching and boring holes in the hill side, all unhappy were the parrots, and the grave turtles squeaked out.
> There were probably sun dials on the top of the

hill, and the "borogoves were afraid that their nests would be undermined. The hill was probably full of the nests of "raths," which ran out squeaking with fear on hearing the "toves" scratching outside . . .[13]

This explanation (written by Carroll at twenty-three) is as good an example of odd juxtapositions, another element of nonsense verse, as can be found. Yet the temptation to repeat the refrain in "The Hunting of the Snark" will further emphasize the point:

> They sought it with thimbles, they sought it with care:
>   They pursued it with forks and hope;
> They threatened its life with a railway-share;
>   They charmed it with smiles and hope.[14]

Strange juxtapositions are evident in many nursery rhymes; in "Hey, Diddle, Diddle" there seems very little connection linking a cow, the moon, a dog, a cat, a fiddle, a dish, and a spoon.

Distortion of language, although related to neulogisms, is found continually as a part of certain kinds of nonsense. Phrases that are literally nonsensical are familiar to any reader of nursery rhymes who may know that "Diddle, diddle, dumpling, my son John" took its beginnings from the cry of the hot-dumpling seller. Such a beginning as "Doodledy, doodledy, doodledy, dan" would appear to have no such origin, nor does Samuel Goodrich's "Higgledy, piggledy, pop!" Counting rhymes provide seemingly nonsensical beginnings for any number of verses we may hear children chanting, unaware that they were originally numbers.

Laura Richards' "Eletelephony" employs distortion of words where even the youngest child would have no trouble recognizing prefix or suffix in "telephant," "telephunk," "telephee," and "telephong." Jack Prelutsky has written of "The Frummick and the Frelly" who eat "jingleberry jelly" and "pinkadoodle pie." Distortion for the sake of end rhyme was a stock-in-trade of Richards, and certainly practiced on a more sophisticated level by Ogden Nash. End-rhyme distortion, alone, however, falls more into the element of word-play than nonsense. Mixing up words is *not* mixing up worlds. It is interesting to note that, although they delighted in various kinds of word-play and neulogisms (from the Scroobious Pip to the Bandersnatch and Jubjub), Lear and Carroll seldom used distorted end rhyme. Theirs was chiefly a nonsense of content, rather than form.

Alliteration is still another tool of the nonsense writer. Used to the nth degree, as in "Peter Piper picked a peck of pickled peppers," it becomes a tongue twister. Jack Prelutsky uses it only a shade more sparingly in his "Flonster Poem":

> The flime devoured the floober
> and the flummie dined on flime,
> the fleemie gulped the flummie down
> in scarcely any time . . .[15]

Lear displays more balanced control in his "Pelican Chorus":

> Ploffskin, Pluffskin, Pelican jee!
> We think no birds as happy as we!
> Plumpskin, Ploshkin, Pelican jill!
> We think so then, and we thought so still![16]

Personification is another tool of the nonsense writer. Not only animals, but trees, eggs, kitchen implements, furniture—indeed, everything may have something to say or do! Laura Richards, in one of her many Lear imitations, wrote about:

> The owl and the eel and the warming-pan,
> They went to call on the soap-fat man.
> The soap-fat man was not within;
> He'd gone to ride on his rolling-pin.
> So they all came back by the way of the town,
> And turned the meeting-house upside down.[17]

The jarring juxtaposition of owl, eel, and warming-pan seems, to me, without control, particularly as their reason for being together has no meaning in terms of the verse. Dennis Lee's Poodle and Grundiboob interact with each other as do dozens of other otherwise inanimate objects. Personification, as X.J. Kennedy conceives of it, is under the tightest control in "Exploding Gravy":

> My mother's big green gravy boat
> Once thought he was a navy boat.
>
> I poured him over my mashed potatoes.
> And out swam seven swift torpedoes.
>
> Torpedoes whizzed and whirred, and—WHAM!
> One bumped smack into my hunk of ham
>
> And blew up with an awful roar,
> Flinging my carrots on the floor . . .[18]

This excellent bit of nonsense, using personification and judicious alliteration, illustrates another tool of the nonsense writer—hyperbole, or exaggeration. Hyperbole is a constant in humorous or funny verse and one of the trademarks of Shel Silverstein, whose work is less nonsensical, to me, and more inclined to zaniness and wild imagination.

The plight of "Sarah Cynthia Sylvia Stout Who Would Not Take the Garbage Out" or "Jimmy Jet and His TV Set" is rooted in the cautionary rhyme. Both have elements of nonsense at the conclusion, but curiously refuse to budge from the world of reality because dislike of carrying out garbage or watching TV are both within range of our own real associations. The concept of garbage reaching from New York to the Golden Gate and Jimmy Jet turning into a TV set is preposterous, and yet we are so mindful of environmental pollution, so aware that all of us may be turning into mental TV sets, that we cannot truly disassociate ourselves. It is almost the same with those poems, written in the first person, where the poet is about to be swallowed up by some imaginary creature, or is writing a poem from inside a lion. It is not the "I" who is nonsensical, such as we find in Lear's limerick characters who do absurd things. The "I" is at the mercy of something or someone else; the irrationality of our own inability to control what happens to us is always omnipresent. Silverstein's verses are, to me, hilariously funny and witty but more in the realm of wild imagination or illusion than nonsense. It is as though he has gone to the place *Where the Sidewalk Ends,* but stops short of taking the one last step to the world of nonsense. It is a very fine line. Silverstein can never quite relinquish the world of reality. The escape is never complete.

Hyperbole is certainly evident in Ian Serraillier's "The Headless Gardener":

> A gardener, Tobias Baird,
> sent his head to be repaired;
> he thought, as nothing much was wrong,
> he wouldn't be without it long.
>
> Ten years he's weeded path and plot,
> a headless gardener, God wot,
> always hoping (hope is vain)
> to see his noddle back again.
>
> Don't pity him for his distress—
> he never sent up his address.[19]

The tools of the nonsense writer are many. Any one of these used to excess may well disturb the balance of a world whose very existence depends on the utmost in careful control.

Nonsense verse is continually changing just as any form of literature must. But some elements remain constant, and none more so than the form, where the lilting beat of the anapest, so often used, makes our heartbeat speed up a bit. Regularity of meter and rhyme assure us that this impossible world is well under the control of a rational mind. It takes a good craftsman to write nonsense verse, one who understands that consonants and assonance must never get too heavy for the subject of nonsense, nor must the meter lose its lightness. Christian Morgenstern's "Porcupine and Porcupina" may give us a clue as to how this works:

A porcupine sat on the lea,
On one quill piping tunefully
  Shalmeiala, shalmeialoo!
His true love, Porcupina,
Came down to nyna-nina
  To his sweet melody,
    Spoonaleea, spoonalya,
    Spoonaleia, loo.

The beast's whole shirt was soon outblown . . .
She said, "How dreadfully strange you've grown"
  Shalmeiala, shalmeialu—,
Then ran off to the neighbor's, Eh!
He, by the brook was washed away
  To a distant pond, alone.
    Lullalee, lullalei,
    Lullaya, loo.
      Too too . . .[20]

Not only the title but the first two lines may prepare us for
nonsense. Porcupines do not normally sit and pipe on their
quills. But the sound of the third line is not that of "hey,
diddle, diddle" or "higgledy, piggledy, pop!" It is not iambic
or anapestic but made up of the falling feet, the dactyl and
trochee. We may pause here and read further, even fooled
by the seeming nonsense of "nyna-nina" or "Spoonaleea,
spoonalya,/Spoonaleia, loo." But the second stanza bursts
upon us with an unmistakable heaviness, both in concept
and rhythm, achieved not only through a series of spondees
but through the assonance of the o and n in "whole,"
"soon," and "outblown." The tragedy is no surprise to us.
Neither was it in Lear's "The Courtship of the Yonghy-

Bonghy-Bò," where the same combination of the vowels came as a warning that here was no nonsense.

Form and sound serve as reliable guideposts for the content of nonsense. They are not foolproof but most often they work well in the hands of the poet. This holds true for all of the elements discussed here. None will suffice by itself, but used in combination by someone able to play the "game," we will be able to escape to the nonsense world.

It is interesting to note that most of those writing nonsense today show control, in meter and rhyme and form, equal to that of Carroll and Lear, although some limerick writers are careless with metrics. The most startling change is in use of the voice; what was primarily narrative in nursery rhyme, Lear, and Carroll has become first-person singular for a number of nonsense writers. Others move between the two voices. Today's nonsense writer injects himself more into his verses, with a number of witty asides. The cautionary rhyme, certainly not the province of nonsense in its original form, has been adopted as a vehicle for nonsense by some. There are even traces of didacticism creeping in, as well as explanations, lest the reader be led astray! Whether any of this is to the betterment of nonsense verse is moot. It does tend to cloud, however, the difference between nonsense on the one hand, and verses merely meant to be amusing, outrageously funny, witty, or simply vehicles for wordplay.

Kornei Chukovsky has written extensively in *From Two to Five* of the need for nonsense, for "topsy-turvies" for the very young, of their universal and "consistent aversion" to "carefully established reality."[21] It is through nonsense, he maintains, that children build their own self-esteem and strengthen their knowledge of reality. Yet nonsense, to me, must also be a release, an adventure and an escape from the rigors of reality for adults as well.

> There was an old person of Rimini
> Who said, "Gracious! Goodness! O Gimini!"
>   When they said, "Please be still!"
>   She ran down a hill
> And was never once heard of at Rimini.[22]

I have often thought it is not so much the children who understand or appreciate the "they" of the Lear limericks as it is the adults. We must all run away, at times, from the "they" who order our feet of clay to move. What better escape than nonsense?

References

1. Edward Lear. "The Jumblies," *Complete Nonsense Book.* New York: Dodd, Mead & Company, 1958.
2. G.K. Chesterton. "Lewis Carroll," *A Handful of Authors.* New York: Sheed & Ward, 1953.
3. Phyllis Greenacre. *Swift and Carroll: A Psychoanalytic Study of Two Lives.* New York: International Universities Press, 1955.
4. Vivian Noakes. *Edward Lear, the Life of a Wanderer.* Boston: Houghton, Mifflin Company, 1969.
5. N.M. Bodecker. "Poundcake from Ealing," *Hurry, Hurry, Mary Dear! and Other Nonsense Poems.* New York: Atheneum Publishers, A Margaret K. McElderry Book, 1976.
6. Richard Wilbur. *Opposites.* New York: Harcourt Brace Jovanovich, Inc., 1973.
7. Lewis Carroll. "Father William," *Alice's Adventures in Wonderland.* New York: Random House, 1946.
8. William Jay Smith. "The Antimacassar and the Ottoman,"

Mr. Smith & Other Nonsense. New York: Delacorte Press, A Seymour Lawrence Book, 1968.

9. Edward Lear. "The Courtship of the Yonghy-Bonghy-Bò," op. cit.
10. Lewis Carroll. "The Walrus and the Carpenter," *Through the Looking-Glass, and What Alice Found There.* New York: Random House, 1946.
11. David McCord. "Pome," *One at a Time.* Boston: Little, Brown, 1974.
12. Lewis Carroll. "Jabberwocky," op. cit.
13. Myra Cohn Livingston, selector. *Poems of Lewis Carroll.* New York: Thomas Y. Crowell Company, 1973.
14. Lewis Carroll. *The Hunting of the Snark.* London: Macmillan and Company, 1876.
15. Jack Prelutsky. "Flonster Poem," *The Snopp on the Sidewalk and Other Poems.* New York: Greenwillow Books, 1977.
16. Edward Lear. "The Pelican Chorus," op. cit.
17. Laura Richards. "The Owl and the Eel and the Warming-Pan," *Tirra-Lirra, Rhymes Old and New.* Boston: Little, Brown, 1902.
18. X.J. Kennedy. "Exploding Gravy," *One Winter Night in August and Other Nonsense Rhymes.* New York: Atheneum Publishers, A Margaret McElderry Book, 1975.
19. Ian Serraillier. "The Headless Gardener," *Thomas and the Sparrow.* London: Oxford University Press, 1951.
20. Christian Morgenstern. "Porcupine and Porcupina," translated by W.D. Snodgrass and Lore Segal, *Gallows Songs.* Ann Arbor, Michigan: University of Michigan Press, 1967.
21. Kornei Chukovsky. *From Two to Five,* translated by Miriam Morton. Berkeley and Los Angeles: University of California Press, 1963.
22. Edward Lear. op. cit.

PRODUCING
THE
BOOKS

Editing Books for
Young People

❧

Ursula Nordstrom

What does an editor of books for young people do? Well, that all depends. It depends on the type of house with which the editor is associated, his or her relationship to the management, the type of management, and the current state of the economy. Above all it depends, of course, on the editor's temperament, stamina, and flexibility. It is not work for someone who demands a structured daily schedule. The editor must be open to new ideas, and must be as available as possible to the creative author and artist and to the department's staff.

An editor may be an acquisition editor, one who approaches someone with a famous name and then turns a possibly unpublishable manuscript over to another editor to try to turn into a book. (This seldom happens in the junior book field, fortunately.) An editor may be someone who works with a manuscript accepted and contracted for by the department head. Ideally, an editor loves creative persons who write and illustrate for children and is also insatiably curious about every single thing concerning anyone who seems to have the slightest drop of talent. Curiosity—intense interest—is very important if tactfully expressed. An editor can be so honestly curious that there will be no hesitancy in asking questions, often intimate personal questions. Of course, the editor must try to figure out which author may be offended by intimate personal questions, and which author may finally be so convinced of the editor's absolutely honest and sensitive curiosity (read *interest*) about every single thing about the author's past, present, and future personal likes, personal hates—indeed, the entire background—that the author will grow to trust the editor. Then the creative person may open up, and sometimes the pearl that has formed around that grain of sand will be discovered. This analogy is banal, and it is banal because it is often true.

Curiosity is not limited to personal inquiry. It is a good idea for an editor to ask questions and keep asking them if there is a place in a manuscript that doesn't seem to be exactly right. There once was an author-artist who was working on the words for a book about a boy named Max who went where the wild things were. At a certain place in the text, toward the end, the author-artist wanted to get Max home again. He couldn't find exactly the right way to say it. He sat in the editor's office and the editor said, "Well, why did Max want to go home?" "I guess he didn't care any more," the author-artist said, "but that's not it." "Well, why do you suppose he did want to go home right at that point?" the editor asked.

The editor kept asking him, and the author-artist didn't get irritated because he realized the editor was trying to help him come out with what was really in his head, deep in his head and heart. But he somehow couldn't quite bring himself to say it. He twisted around and grinned in self-derision. "He just wanted to be with his *mommy,*" he said, in a mock-babyish way, "but I can't say *that.*" "Well, you can't say just that," the editor agreed. "But really, why did he want to go home right then?"

There were a few more joking tries that both shook off. Then the author-artist looked away and said again tentatively, very softly, "Well, he wanted to be where someone loved him best of all, but I couldn't really say *that.*" "Why not?" said the editor. "It's absolutely perfect, and it is exactly what you mean, but for some strange Sendakian reason you couldn't bring yourself to say it. But it is perfect." And it was, and it is. And it came out of the author-artist's head and heart. The editor just kept asking questions until Sendak could bring himself to admit it, bring himself to say the actual words.

Editorial interest reaches even beyond submitted projects. When a dear and valued author is between manuscripts, either blocked completely or working on a new idea, it is necessary for the editor in some cases to make a friendly phone call, or drop a friendly note, to ask how things are going: "Not to pressure you. Just wanted to be in touch and see how you are." Some authors want and need that. It makes them feel loved. But some authors absolutely hate such inquiries, consider them prying and nagging, and tell the editor so in no uncertain words.

Some authors and artists want and need a firm deadline for the delivery of manuscripts or illustrations. They consider a deadline a great help. Others, though given a deadline, absolutely detest being reminded of it, no matter how gently and, again, consider the editor to be nagging and thus making creative work practically impossible. It is important but not always easy to know the difference.

One occupational hazard for an editor is to be cast by the author or artist in the role of mother or father. Often an author welcomes suggestions for possible improvement of a manuscript. But sometimes if an editor suggests a lot of cutting, or the strengthening of a characterization, the author feels mother is nagging and really means the equivalent of "Now get this room cleaned up at once!" The finest authors have their young selves emotionally and easily available to them, and that doesn't always make for an emotionally mature and reasonable person. (It doesn't do a bit of harm if the editor is a little nuts, too.)

Often an author will start a manuscript with a certain idea for a book but wander away from what the original idea was. Here an editor can tactfully try to bring the author back to the original vision. And always the editor must be sure the author knows that the editor wants what is in the author's head, not what is in the editor's head. The editor can point to places where the action drags, where the author has included an extraneous passage just for the sheer self-indulgent pleasure of writing it. One editor, reading an exciting chapter in a manuscript about a mother who had mislaid her small child in a shopping mall, was treated, as the mother hunted in panic for the child, to a fascinating, meticulous, and endless description of the shopping mall. The author had absolutely loved writing two marvelous pages about the sights, sounds, smells, and ambience of a shopping mall. But of course it would have stopped the action and the readers cold. In a case like this, an editor can be helpful in pointing out affectionately but *firmly* that no one cares at that point for details about a shopping mall. Please find that child! (And rest assured that the two fine pages about the shopping mall will eventually be used to excellent purpose in a later book by that author.)

If an editor thinks a manuscript seems to drag, that the action seems too slow, it is relatively easy to spot the problem on a manuscript for nine-year-olds or older. "That eighth chapter seems to be a bit slow. Won't you reread it and see if it can't be shortened?" Or "The character of the grandfather doesn't seem convincing here. Would he have bawled out the boy in quite such a hostile fashion?" But when it comes to suggesting possible cuts in a picture-book manuscript, or in a book of poems, the job of the editor is much more difficult and full of danger. I do not exaggerate. Once an editor told the author of a book of poems that they were all simply wonderful, varied, full of humor, full of emotion. But "perhaps you could omit a few of the poems? The book does seem a little long. What do you think?"

It did not take long for the editor to find out. "What do I think!" the author exploded. "I think that, gosh darn it," (not his exact words) "I think you love to say cut, cut, cut. I bet that if Moses had brought you his Commandments you'd have said, 'Oh, thank you, Mr. Moses. I like these tablets very much. These are good Commandments. But aren't twelve a bit too many? Couldn't you cut these Commandments to ten?' " At this the editor roared with laughter: she had thought that perhaps bits of *Moby Dick* might have been shortened but had never considered trying to help Moses work on the Commandments. Her appreciation so pleased the poet that he thriftily used the general idea in his next adult book.

When a picture book is in rough dummy form, the

editor will go through it to see how the pages turn. Perhaps a word or a phrase placed at the bottom of a page should be transferred to the top of the following page. Sometimes such a seemingly minute change can be dramatic in improving the pace of the book, and thus in holding the child's interest. Going through the dummy, the editor and the author may see that some few words are not really needed any more, that the drawings will take care of what a few of the words in the original manuscript indicated. This is a difficult moment for the editor and a tense one for the author, every word of whose manuscript is precious. Some examples are still too painful for this editor (not to mention the authors) to discuss. But every word in a picture book is or should be perfect. The really great and lasting picture books are the closest art form to the finest lyric poetry.

Unless the author is also the artist, the editor has to be sensitive to the problem of using exactly the right artist for a particular manuscript. This is not always easy. One editor worked on a picture book with Author A and Artist B. The relationship between A and B was one of terminal Hate. B actually did a beautiful set of pictures, and when the final book was published none of the blood shed in the editor's office showed at all. Sometimes, of course, there is mutual respect and appreciation and great creative contribution to and from author and artist. But when there is friction it is the editor who must try to make things a little easier for both creative persons. It is said that Lewis Carroll was highly critical of some of Tenniel's pictures for *Alice,* pictures that now seem perfect.

One editor, when hostile author and hostile artist arrived for a session over the artist's sketches, tried to make a little (very little!) joke about the increasing friction by saying, "Well, now, we have a beautiful book being developed here, and any disagreements can be quickly settled." Whereupon the editor placed a tiny pair of perfect leather boxing gloves on the desk with a nervous and hopefully mollifying smile. The "little joke" turned out to be not little, but invisible. Anyhow, one of the editor's most interesting responsibilities is to find the right artist for the work, to be sure that the author approves of the selection, and then to see that eventually the collaboration results in a picture book good enough for children.

When a fine artist does a set of illustrations for a book, particularly if the pictures are in full color, there is great tension for the artist and the editor while the plates are being made and when the proofs are pulled. If the budget allows (and ideally it always should), the printer sends a set of proofs to the editor or the production manager to go over with the artist and let them indicate necessary corrections. "Register bad here." "Black line in corner too heavy, as marked." "Blue is too pale." And so forth. The tension a fine artist feels over the reproduction of illustrations cannot possibly be exaggerated. Infrequently the first set of proofs is perfect and everyone is relieved and delighted. However, an editor may often receive a set of proofs that needs perhaps minor corrections, but that on the whole are a pleasant surprise to the editor and the production person. And the editor *thinks* that on the whole the artist will be pleased.

In a case like this an editor might telephone the nervous artist (who picks up on the first ring!) and say, "Well, the proofs are here. Can you come right away and go over them with us?" "Oh, my God," cries the artist. "How are they?

Are they awful? What do you think?" The editor need not say, "They are really quite good. You'll be pleased. We just need minor corrections." The editor might rather want to say, "Well, they're not perfect, but they can be made much better." "Oh God, you mean they are terrible?" "No, they're *not* terrible. They do need correction. Now don't get so upset. After all, this is why we pay extra, to have these proofs pulled so we can all go over them and get them right."

By the time the artist arrives within the hour to look at the proofs, he is prepared for something much further from perfection than the rather good proofs with which he is presented. The artist is therefore pleasantly surprised and relieved and says, "Why, these are much better than I thought they would be. I'm really pleased." This little editorial deception thus makes the artist happier than the artist had expected to be. And, after all, making authors and artists happier than they expected to be is one of the things an editor gets up in the morning to try to do.

The editorial/artistic relationship can't always be personal. An editor may have started in a department so small that the editor was able to read all the submitted manuscripts personally. But as a department grows the editor/publisher must be as perceptive and sensitive in the selection of readers, assistant editors, and associate editors as in the publication of manuscripts. The editor/publisher (and author!) may often be at the mercy of the first or second reader. An editor/publisher is wise, if time forbids the personal reading of every manuscript, at least to try to find the time to read the reports submitted by the reader and glance at the actual manuscript to see if the original reader has caught or missed the true flavor of the work. If even that is impossible, an effort must be made by the editor/publisher to be as close and available as time and temperament permit to those who read the manuscripts. They must be alert to a paragraph, a page, that shows freshness and originality—and then new talent can be encouraged.

Readers and editors are not always perceptive to quality in all the various kinds of manuscripts. The reader may react creatively to young adult novels but be unable to visualize a picture book from a one- or two-page script. Once there was something about a brief report, derisively dismissing a manuscript, that puzzled the editor. The report said, "Here are a couple of pages by a lady who thinks a tree is nice. Birds sit in it. Cows lie under it. Who cares?" The editor has always been thankful that the manuscript was immediately reread and published as *A Tree Is Nice* by Janice May Udry, and illustrated by Marc Simont, who then won the Caldecott Medal for his illustrations. Janice went on to write many other books, including *Let's Be Enemies* and *Moon Jumpers,* both illustrated by Maurice Sendak. An interesting footnote is that the reader who dismissed the "tree is nice" idea came rushing into the editor's office a little later crying, "You have GOT to take this manuscript." It was a long book for an older age group, and it became a prize-winner and the first of many fine books by a hitherto unpublished author. So some good readers and editors will have blind spots for potential picture books, some for longer books. Some fortunate editors can perceive talent in both.

An editor of books for young people must not only help the creators turn talent into books but also protect the department's turf. These days the junior book department is usually a separate entity, with its own staff, its own advertising and promotion group, its own production manager. It usually has its own figures on inventory, royalty outstanding, advanced royalties on manuscripts never delivered, and profit and loss statements. If the bottom line shows a good profit, that's great, and it is also—alas—an important time for the junior book editor to look out for the department's continued independence.

One has heard (not often, but one *has* heard) of the heads of adult trade departments who have suddenly thought to themselves, and repeated this thought to the top management, "Hey, why don't we put the junior books and the adult trade into one department? Really, that would make more sense. They're all trade books, actually. The same salesmen sell them, and I just think the junior books and their profit should now become part of the regular adult trade department." (Note: Throughout the above, the publishing head of the adult trade department probably referred to junior books as "juvies," which is salt in an easily opened wound.)

Well, when this happens, it is time for the editor to fight for the department's turf. It is important for those departmental figures to be kept separately, and to show that the department is making money. (If they don't show a profit, of course, the conversation between the adult trade editor and top management will never take place.) If the department shows a healthy profit, top management must admit that "they must be doing something right" and keep hands off.

The "bottom line" phrase irritates a lot of editors, but it is extremely important to keep that profit healthy. In a book column, on a business page, appeared this statement: "The bottom line impacted negatively." Such a poetic way of explaining why a department was being liquidated. Junior book departments are best run by one person, responsible for the publishing of the books *and* for the bottom line of the department's profit and loss sheet.

An editor responsible for the bottom line as well as the activities of the junior book department is often in a tough situation. An editor can be sitting in the office talking to a valued and temperamental—and often screaming—author, trying to placate, explain, express love and understanding to that distressed and miserable person. The editor will try to appear calm and reassuring, but at that very moment may be fifteen minutes late to an important financial meeting to go over the inventory, the unearned royalty advances, the general overhead of the department. So, when and if the unhappy author is made somewhat happier, the editor arrives late at the important meeting, with a splitting headache and a muttered reminder to the bruised self that no one ever promised any editorial rose gardens.

Above all, the junior books editor must remember the young person for whom the book is intended. Editors try to look out for a writer's occasional temptation to toss in a little adult-appearing touch, a sort of patronizing adult wink over the child's shoulder to another adult. It is the wise editor who will catch that and warn gently, "Oh, there. Stop winking at some stupid adult to get a cheap smile. The child will be aware of it and may be put off." Between the creative author and the creative young reader stand so many adults —editors, reviewers, librarians, parents (oh, parents!)—sifting their own adult reactions to books meant for brand-new people. Ultimately, it is the child to whom editors must be responsible through their fascinating, often maddening, but greatly rewarding profession.

Publishers and Librarians

∽

Mimi Kayden

Once upon a time, many years ago, there were not very many children's librarians, but there were even fewer publishers with an editor whose true interest was children's books. Louise Seaman Bechtel started a children's book department at Macmillan in 1919, and by the beginning of the 1930s there were no more than four or five such editors in the New York area. It was only natural that with Anne Carroll Moore, the pioneer children's services coordinator available just a few blocks away at The New York Public Library, the dialogue began. In time, the group of librarians and editors enlarged, friendships multiplied, travel became easier, and conventions abounded. Eventually that small network grew into a transcontinental sharing of purpose that is unique in both the publishing and institutional field. And at times the distinctions blur. Children's librarians have become children's book editors or book marketing people. Publishers, too, have become librarians, but not in so great a number.

Before the end of the sixties, when decentralization and urban decay took their toll, the lines of communication became much clearer, for the big urban library systems were the postgraduate training ground of children's librarians all over the country. The New York Public Library, Boston Public, and Enoch Pratt in Baltimore, to name just a few, sent recruiters each spring to the major library schools to encourage the best future librarians to apply for work in their library systems. Acting like apprentices, the young librarians would work for two years or longer, practicing their skills in the most prestigious systems, gathering wide-ranging experiences, and then moving on to opportunities elsewhere in the smaller libraries of both the United States and Canada.

This system helped publishers keep tabs on what was going on in their major market. An editor could find out what the trends were, and therefore what type of book would sell, by checking with the children's coordinators in Pittsburgh or Los Angeles or Philadelphia. And a few advance reading copies sent to key opinion makers or systems would place the book on a recommended reading list, insuring that the title would sell for many years to come. Unlike adult books, which could go out of print within a year of publication, children's books rarely did so if they obtained the necessary recommendations. It was commonplace for a children's book to stay in print for five, ten, and even fifteen years.

More than for any other type of publishing, the children's book market has been well defined. The publishers haven't had to direct their promotion at the ultimate consumer as is necessary with trade adult books, how-to books, or textbooks. Children rarely buy the books they read themselves. Adults preselect juveniles, purchase them, and sometimes even censor them. Today, in 1981, libraries still account for 75 to 90 percent of all the higher priced, hardcover books sold, and it is only through the efforts of the publisher and the librarian together that the books reach their readership.

When I started in publishing a little over twenty years ago, there were almost as few library promotion people as there were children's book editors thirty years earlier. Most of the contact with librarians was through the editors. The launching of Sputnik in 1957 and the enactment of Title III of the National Defense Education Act shortly thereafter, with its emphasis on supplementary educational materials, caused the scene to change radically.

Most people in publishing will tell you that their careers have been based to a large part on luck. They just happened to be in the right place at the right time, and that is what happened to me. In 1958 I was a temporary worker at Harper and when I had a spare moment I typed up labels for sending the review books to librarians. As I went up in the elevator one day I asked why the names weren't put on stencils rather than have them typed up individually each season? Different libraries don't always get the same books was the reply. I suggested keying the labels with an AJ for all juvenile, SJ for selected juvenile, etc. Somebody must have overheard and the next thing I knew, I was regarded as an expert in the library promotion field.

I guess stranger things have happened, but I was lucky and got in on the first wave of library promotion people to come upon the new publishing scene. We were young. We weren't paid very much. We weren't important. And all of that was okay because if we were expendable enough for others not to worry about us, we were able to go out and find out what librarians thought about the books we published, what they wanted of books that were not yet published, what their buying patterns were, and how we could best help in supplying catalogs, brochures, bindings, posters, authors, exhibits, whatever. In other words, we could do no harm and we hoped we could do a lot of good!

In 1963 NDEA was expanded and money began to flow into the children's book coffers. It was followed by the dramatic changes brought by the Elementary and Secondary Education Act. School libraries had always existed but, except for the southeastern United States, they were mainly in the high schools or they were small collections staffed by volunteers. Now they began to develop nationwide. Heads of publishing houses took a new look at what had been before mostly a backroom, quiet-but-steady way of making money. The library promotion field mushroomed.

We took road trips on the new interstate highway system, taking in state and regional library conventions, calling on librarians in their home offices to express our interest in what they did, how they did it, and whether or not a review copy of everything on our list might make their selection process easier. Do you have a reviewing system? How do you select your books? Do you buy multiple copies? How many librarians or libraries participate in your setup? And how much do you spend on children's books from federal, state, and local monies? Sample-copy lists, which at the start of the sixties were between one hundred and two hundred names, grew to be five hundred or more names. And just in case we missed someone or someone missed us, we mailed out newsletters, promotion pieces, bookmarks, and posters by the thousands.

Today, library promotion (in a new incarnation, library marketing or children's book marketing) is a readily identifiable segment of most publishing houses. It is not just one person or one library promotion specialist and a secretary as it was originally. Instead it is a whole department incorporating copywriters, designers, and production specialists, and it is responsible for providing the knowledge of how to reach the marketplace as well as what materials and methods best get the books to the bookstores, libraries, institutions —and children.

According to the Association of American Publishers' latest report, publishers in 1978 spent an average of 5.2 percent of their net income for children's books on marketing. Thus, if sales were expected to be $1,000,000 for the year, the publisher could spend $52,000 to promote those titles. That sum would have to cover the cost of any direct mail or promotion piece, such as seasonal catalogs of new titles, a backlist catalog, or a "graded list" that might be produced as either a separate catalog or included in the seasonal catalog; newsletters; brochures on authors important to the list, special subjects such as Chinese history and culture, or series such as beginning readers. It would include the cost of "point of sales" materials, such as counter displays and dumps that hold a number of the same title together for bookstore arrangements, window streamers, and posters. And it would also include the cost of reproductions of illustrations from books in poster form, bookmarks, mobiles, and other freebies the publisher has available upon request.

Under publicity, the same $52,000 would have to cover the cost of the review copies sent to libraries and newspaper and magazine reviewers, the cost of releases, author tours, and so on. And under advertising it would have to include the cost of ads in *Publishers Weekly, Booklist, School Library Journal, Horn Book, The New York Times, Language Arts,* or whatever.

Nor is that the end. From the same $52,000, marketing departments have to arrange for conventions and exhibits, attending such national conferences as the American Library Association convention or the International Reading Association convention, and they must send books to those meetings they cannot attend in person, such as the meetings of the National Science Teachers or the American Alliance of Health, Physical Education and Recreation.

Obviously, with just $52,000 to spend per $1,000,000 in income, publishers can't do all of those things and they must pick or choose among them. A realistic assessment of the book's potential audience and where the book will sell is paramount.

The purpose of this, of course, is to reach the ultimate reader: the child. We may know, for example, that children will gobble up a book on worms and worm habits if they can get their hands on it, but it seems unlikely that anyone will buy it as a gift in a bookstore. How do we promote it? First of all, we do for this book what we do for every title on the list: we make up a "Title Information" sheet for the sales staff, which not only gives some information on the book and the author but also some tips on why we are publishing it, how the book differs from others in the field, what will interest readers in the book, how it can be used successfully in the classroom, how many illustrations there are and what they add to the book, and what the author's other accomplishments are.

Next we put the book in a list ad or a catalog of books to be published and send out review copies to the principal review media and the major public and school libraries around the country. We also send the book to the American Association for the Advancement of Science, *Scientific American, Appraisal,* the NSTA journals; and maybe, if time and money permit, we send press releases to local groups interested in worms, possibly having some fun talking about a Diet of Worms, the Royal Order of Wyrms, or even "Bookworms I Have Known." We even try to notify all of the author's friends. The possibilities are endless and, whether a book is a literary classic, a first effort by a potentially fine author, an addition to an established series, or a departure from the regular publishing program, the job of promoting a book is never finished. There is always something more that could be done and should be done, but won't be. Money and, in a case like this especially, time are limiting factors.

Over the years, the erosion of tax dollars, the decline in the birthrate, inflation, and the scarcity of materials have had their effect on publishers and librarians. In libraries circulation has declined, budgets have been cut or failed to keep up with inflation, and schools have been consolidated. Publishers, because of inflationary manufacturing, overhead, and promotion costs, are no longer able to print a modest 4,000 to 6,000 copies of a black-and-white illustrated book profitably. We need a larger market to justify larger printings. While we used to concentrate on the library market almost exclusively, we have had to widen our vision to include reading consultants, teachers of English, science and social science instructors, preschool and day care center volunteers, and finally, parents and bookstores. That is why library promotion became marketing: we had to look at what had become a much wider area of interest and had to be able to spend whatever monies or time or talent we had in a much more circumspect way.

There is something very nice about working in these lean years. There is a pride that develops in being able to accomplish—having to accomplish—more with less. A sense of professionalism takes hold that is enhanced by working with librarians, educators, and other publishers who are trying to reach the same goals. Books are a business, but it seems to be unlike any other, since we are not strictly buyers and sellers nor are we in direct competition with one another. Between 2,000 and 3,000 new children's books are published each year. Some fail, more succeed, and a few become perennial favorites. Publishers do sell and librarians do buy, but we work together to make these successes, sending information out, feeding reviews back, and trying to reach the child. It seems to be a never-ending process because there are always new and growing readers and always a new list in a new year to look forward to. We always hope that things will be better. If this way of working together continues, and determination and dedication count, things undoubtedly will be.

UNDERSTANDING
THE
BOOKS

Innocence & Experience: A Critical Paradox

❧

Betsy Hearne

innocent: 1a: free from guilt or sin esp. through lack of knowledge of evil: BLAMELESS b: harmless in effect or intention; *also:* CANDID c: free from legal guilt or fault; *also:* LAWFUL d: lacking something: DESTITUTE 2a: ARTLESS, INGENUOUS b: IGNORANT
experienced: made skillful or wise through observation of or participation in a particular activity or in affairs generally: PRACTICED
Webster's New World Dictionary

Steady involvement with adult literature is essential for perspective on the study of children's books. The truth of this hit home once more when a recent reading of the poetry in William Blake's *Songs of Innocence and Experience* stimulated my realization that the paradox of innocence versus experience is the very crux of the problem I have had in becoming a critic and in maturing as a critic.

Most librarians and reviewers face the same dilemma during their first years of evaluation and selection: how to make and articulate sound book judgments without literary experience. What does one do with one's innocence, or ignorance, while acquiring that experience? And once experienced, how does one retain enough innocence to see freshly, without a jaded eye?

Listen to these representative statements of innocence and experience from Blake. They are counterpoint visions of the same thing:

For Mercy has a human heart,
Pity a human face,
And Love, the human form divine,
And Peace, the human dress.
                              "The Divine Image," *Songs of Innocence*

∽

Cruelty has a Human Heart
And Jealousy a Human Face;
Terror the Human Form Divine,
And Secrecy the Human Dress.
                              "A Divine Image," *Songs of Experience*

∽

When the voices of children are heard on the green
And laughing is heard on the hill,
My heart is at rest within my breast
And everything else is still.

"Then come home, my children, the sun is gone down
And the dews of night arise;
Come, come, leave off play, and let us away
Till the morning appears in the skies."

"No, no, let us play, for it is yet day
And we cannot go to sleep;
Besides, in the sky the little birds fly
And the hills are all cover'd with sheep."

"Well, well, go and play till the light fades away
And then go home to bed."
The little ones leaped and shouted and laugh'd
And all the hills echoed.
                    "Nurse's Song," *Songs of Innocence*

                    ∽

When the voices of children are heard on the green
And whisp'rings are in the dale,
The days of my youth rise fresh in my mind,
My face turns green and pale.

Then come home, my children, the sun is gone down,
And the dews of night arise;
Your spring and your day are wasted in play,
And your winter and night in disguise.
                    "Nurse's Song," *Songs of Experience*

In studying Blake's poetry I had less sense of possible resolution to the paradox of innocence and experience than of their forceful description as inescapable cycles one goes through, whether happily or sadly. What does seem to be profoundly missing from his verses as well as from many of us, whether we are just starting out or becoming jaded, is some sort of balance between innocence and experience.

As a beginning critic, I had both the gift and the drawback of naiveté, of belief. Naiveté kept the terms of criticism that I memorized in school from coming between me and an immediate experience of the book. Naiveté kept me from prejudgment—and also from judgment. Yet suddenly and inescapably, it was my duty as a professional critic to make judgments. Somehow the intellectualized categories I had learned in theory had to be translated in body, into the actual experiencing of the book. I couldn't stop with a quick, silent, personal reaction.

At first I felt simply inadequate. I *knew* I was a sucker for books. I *didn't* know what to do with all those books that appeared on my desk demanding evaluation in a journal that came under public scrutiny every two weeks. I yearned for the strength of definite decisions. It has taken me a long time to learn to value the very hesitation with which I make decisions about a book. It has also taken me a long time to incorporate firmly the theoretical categories of formal education into an organic understanding.

I'm glad now that I did not trust theories when they were unripe in my mind, although that required feeling the pain of inadequacy. It is important to learn to admit when one truly does not know how to react, for that is a kind of innocence. Innocence can bring with it a fresh way of looking at things that sometimes involves discoveries others do not make because, instead of admitting lack of knowledge, they have accepted assumptions and acted on them before tempering them with their own individual experience. It is that individual experience that makes creative critics, that tempering and balancing of the known and the admittedly unknown. Therein lies discovery.

If I were starting over again, I would give myself this advice: Don't be afraid of knowledge. You need all you can get. Don't be afraid of a lack of knowledge. It leads to questioning. The combination is a great strength, particularly when shored by the confidence to feel one's way through time to a resolution.

I do not nourish literary naiveté, but I certainly honor it. I don't nourish disillusionment, but I honor it as well. For naiveté can bring surprise as well as shock; and disillusionment can bring understanding as well as cynicism. One has a choice of conclusions in the meeting of innocence and experience. We know this from the hope that has emerged even in the most desperate of situations, such as children's reactions to concentration camps, surely one of the most extreme encounters of innocence with experience. To use a less dramatic example, each of our own childhoods suffered a point when one moment we saw through a glass darkly and the next, face to face, that anything could happen. It is the same in the world of books.

My own balance of innocence and experience in critical evaluation leans toward charity, perhaps because at a crucial point charity was shown me; or at another, charity was not shown me; or perhaps a combination of the two.

Let us take an example of the several possible ways of looking at a book. In November, 1978, *Kirkus* reviewed a book called *Displaced Person* by Marie Bloch:

> Although Bloch is not half bad at describing Germany in its death-rattle days or the sub-subsistence level life of the refugees, the rather startling paradox of the Reich as refuge is never explored or, for that matter, even commented upon by any of the characters. Still more disturbing, the one and only scene involving concentration-camp survivors pictures them as whining

stool pigeons ready to report the refugees to Soviet authorities. Evidently the only kind of dehumanization which concerns Bloch is the Communist kind—yet Stefan's turnabout from stolid little Stalinist to mature civil libertarian is so perfunctory that even as a rites-of-passage story this doesn't seem worth the trek.

Six months later, a small, noncommittal notice appeared and the same book was re-reviewed from an entirely different perspective:

Adult readers who discern a foreshadowing of the troubles East-European immigrants have encountered in America will discover, in the author's afterword, that they're not mistaken; but the book has sufficient fictional integrity and historical authenticity to override any programmatic intent. . . . If the Soviet threat is more pervasive than the Nazi menace, that's a matter of circumstance; throughout, Bloch is careful to have her characters point out parallels between the two. And the message, effectively embodied in Stefan, is that the internalization of repression is a greater danger than its outward expression.

Meanwhile, I had reviewed the book without having seen either *Kirkus* review, but having gone through some unsettling thought and discussion about the strong and weak points of Bloch's work:

In spite of an undistinguished writing style, Bloch has succeeded in portraying Stefan as an individual and as a victim of massive historical forces. His pain and con-

fusion will add to readers' thoughts on a war that has
not often been shown from this point of view.

In the case of the *Kirkus* reviews, the same critical journal—one must assume the same anonymous reviewer—gave
the same book two entirely different readings: one open or
responsive and one closed or disbelieving—one innocent
and one, in my opinion, *over* experienced. There are two sides
to the willing suspension of disbelief. One is the *writer's*
ability to make the reader believe and the other is the *reader's*
ability to respond. That is not to say that the *Kirkus* critic is
any less of a critic than I, but to say firmly and with great
conviction that I as a critic see *differently* than the first *Kirkus*
critic and know why and wherefore. While in this case the
critic's lens was refocused, that is a rare occurrence.

Generally I must have faith in my own balance as being
best, without denying the authenticity of another balance.
That in itself is a matter of confidence in my blend of innocence and experience, and all critics must find it for themselves in face of disagreement with other critics.

If allowed, experience turns innocent uncertainty into
open-mindedness. Of course, lack of knowledge does not
necessarily mean uncertainty. Lack of knowledge can sometimes carry great conviction, for right or wrong. But that
conviction in the instincts of innocence, foolhardy as it may
be, is often what makes people create something out of
nothing, whether they are writers or critics. They are making
ideas not out of something already known, but drawing
from the unknown and then molding it by known skills.
Both the unknown and the known must coexist for creative
thoughts to converge.

It may be valuable, but it is not creative, to read and summarize another's knowledge. That knowledge must be the beginning of the unknown, the jumping-off place into the realm of a new unknown, which carries uncertainty of destination.

To venture the unknown takes time and space that is not already organized into a destination. Children who are not booked into productivity tend to have the kind of space to approach books that critics need to relearn for creative thinking. Terms like *plot* and *characterization* are only half, a kind of final organization of thoughts that have sprung from the actual experience of fictional people and what happens to them. *Color* and *texture* are terms necessary to the critic, but they are only half of looking, the experienced half. The innocent half is absorbed by the wave of blue or red washing over one, the fingerpaint stickiness of it all, the dog's eyes—or perhaps flipping the pages because there is nothing to absorb, and the word for emptiness has not yet formulated itself from the child's store of knowledge.

This raises the question of children's taste and their sometimes astounding lack of it. The exact same balance may be found in adults, yet the great difference between children and adults is experience, of one kind or another. Innocence—or lack of experience—does, as we have seen, actually have a contribution to make in judging books; but it is definitely limiting if it is not eventually accompanied by knowledge. Sometimes that knowledge comes from education and sometimes simply from living.

Innocence is a clean slate and experience a slate written. Experience varies, but innocence is always the same. Innocence is unknowing, while experience is knowing something. Many believe a critic's function is based entirely on experience, or knowledge. But it is that fundamental balance between innocence and experience, between knowing and unknowing, that distinguishes mature from immature, critic from child. The child must learn to be critical, and the critic must learn to be childlike.

Artists struggle for the same balance between knowing and unknowing. The dichotomy between artist and critic as innocent and experienced is a false one based on the assumption that one is creative and the other academic. Both can be creative, and whatever is creative depends on this balance between knowing and unknowing. One without the other is dead. You have read dead criticism and you have read dead art.

Either innocence or experience can lead to wisdom; on the other hand, either innocence or experience may lead to blindness and distrust. But the highest synthesis of innocence and experience is creative awareness in any endeavor. One without the other is off-balance.

For example, a child looks for the first time at an airplane flying overhead and sees a miracle. An adult looks for the umpteenth time at an airplane flying overhead and pays no attention. Somewhere between marvel and technical knowledge lies true awareness.

Listening to music is a rich emotional experience for the uninitiated, but being able to distinguish, through study, the effects of each instrument can deepen the total impact. A child and an adult looking at a picture book together each have advantages and disadvantages by virtue of their innocence and experience. The more they learn from each other, the more complete the experience will be for both. The adult will begin to pore over details without setting a time limit and the child will learn to discriminate between what is worth poring over and what is not.

Experience is a function of time. The acquisition of taste is a function of experience. But it does not follow that time leads to the acquisition of taste without that balance I have mentioned. There *are* differences between children and adults: what does that mean to innocence and experience in criticism of the two different literatures? Mainly it can be summed up in this approach to a book, whether it is for children or adults: Read like a child, freshly; think like an adult, fully.

Children's innocence is ruthless. They won't read anything they don't like; yet what they like may be anything! The adult's experience knows a shade or two of difference: the difficulties of creation, the complexities of the human condition, the patience of delayed gratification. Adults will read anything, though they may not like it.

Tolkien speaks of the difference between child and adult in his critical essay "Tree and Leaf":

> I do not deny that there is truth in Andrew Lang's words (sentimental though they may sound): "He who would enter into the Kingdom of Faerie should have the heart of a little child." For that possession is necessary to all high adventure, into kingdoms both less and far greater than Faerie. But humility and innocence— these things "the heart of a child" must mean in such a context—do not necessarily imply an uncritical wonder, nor indeed an uncritical tenderness. Chesterton once remarked that the children in whose company he

saw Maeterlinck's *Blue Bird* were dissatisfied "because it did not end with a Day of Judgement, and it was not revealed to the hero and the heroine that the Dog had been faithful and the Cat faithless." "For children," he says, "are innocent and love justice; while most of us are wicked and naturally prefer mercy."

If we use *child* in a good sense (it has also legitimately a bad one) we must not allow that to push us into the sentimentality of only using *adult* or *grown-up* in a bad sense (it has also legitimately a good one). The process of growing older is not necessarily allied to growing wickeder, though the two do often happen together. Children are meant to grow up, and not to become Peter Pans. Not to lose innocence and wonder, but to proceed on the appointed journey: that journey upon which it is certainly not better to travel hopefully than to arrive, though we must travel hopefully if we are to arrive. But it is one of the lessons of fairystories (if we can speak of the lessons of things that do not lecture) that on callow, lumpish, and selfish youth peril, sorrow, and the shadow of death can bestow dignity, and even sometimes wisdom.[1]

In approaching books on a daily practical basis, how does one balance knowledge and ignorance, knowing and unknowing art, knowing and unknowing literature, knowing and unknowing children? How does one deal with the kind of random samples one tends to run into in life—not "bad" books or "good" books, but simply books one has trouble approaching for some reason of art, literature, or reader?

I would open up the process of judgment by finding

how to balance the elements of innocence and experience; how one element educates the other; how formal criticism has nothing to do with it and yet does; how the critic's inner child fits in, along with the child down the street, or even the child in the newspaper article one reads over breakfast coffee. School comes at a young age, but education often does not come till one is older. The difference is the ability to balance innocence and experience, knowing which to trust when.

Blake's last line in "Holy Thursday" is a sincere ending to an ironic poem, leavening some of his more judgmental indictments. It illuminates a feeling that I have found to be a nightlight guiding me through the darker confusions of both my innocence and my experience as a critic making judgments among thousands of books for thousands of the relatively helpless people known as children. Whether you do or don't know the next step critically, "Then cherish pity, lest you drive an angel from your door." An open mind hears each book knocking on its door.

1. J.R.R. Tolkien, "Tree and Leaf," *The Tolkien Reader* (New York: Ballantine, 1966), pp. 66–67.

The Reviewing
of Children's Books

∽

John Rowe Townsend

This essay will concern itself with the principles of children's book reviewing as I see them: with the nature and purpose of the art, rather than with the analysis of actual reviews and reviewing media. I shall also say something about the qualities to be desired in reviewers and about the role of the review editor. Most of my observations will apply both to newspapers and general periodicals on the one hand and to specialist children's book publications on the other. The principles, I believe, are much the same in both cases. Here and there, however, I shall draw attention to some differences of approach and emphasis.

For the present purpose I define "reviewing" as critical or appreciative contemporaneous writing about new books in periodical publications. The key phrase I think is *contemporaneous* writing about *new* books. If it isn't contemporaneous, if it isn't about new books, then whatever it may be it's not reviewing. Reviewing comes close on the heels of publication, though not always as close as might be wished. It doesn't normally allow, and is not intended to allow, for long and leisurely consideration, for second and third and fourth thoughts, and for adjustment to the perspectives of time.

What are the functions of reviewing? Here are a few of them, not necessarily in order of importance.

Reviewing seeks to recognize new work of merit. It is the first of the series of siftings and evaluations and reevaluations that determine whether a book has a place on the literary map, and if so, what place, and how long it will retain that place. It may well be pointed out that children's books are for children and that the map of children's literature is of very little interest to children themselves; this is true, but the map has a great deal to do with what will become known to parents, teachers, and librarians, and therefore with what will be recommended to or put before children.

Secondly, and in a sense at the other extreme from this literary function, reviewing is part of the process by which books are published and distributed. Most book review periodicals, and book review pages in general publications, are supported by book advertising. Publishers support book pages with their advertising, and send copies of books for review, because they hope for publicity, for recommendation, for quotations they can use in blurbs and advertisements and promotion. There is nothing corrupt in this, any more than there is in the fact that newspapers and most magazines depend upon advertising for their existence anyway; but we may as well recognize it as a fact of life. If there were no book advertisements, no review copies sent out, then far fewer books would be brought to public notice.

This function as part of the distribution process can of course be looked at from the other end, the consumer's end; and the third function of reviewing can be seen as being to provide a consumer guide for potential buyers of books. Reviewers, in fact, rightly regard themselves as having a duty to the public rather than to the publishers. Publishers tend to think that all their geese are swans. It is part of the job of the reviewer and review editor to sort out the swans from the geese.

Fourth, and never to be forgotten, reviewing is a branch of journalism. This statement applies even to reviewing in specialist periodicals, but obviously applies most strongly to reviewing in newspapers and general magazines. What a reviewer writes will form part of the contents of the publication and the editors hope it will interest a large number of their readers, many of whom will never for a moment consider actually buying a copy of the book under review. The reviewer has a function as a contributor of readable material, as a stimulator of thought, which will be at least as important in the editors' eyes as assessing the relative merits of books. This may be a pity; it encourages the well-known reviewing heresy of writing to the greater glory of oneself rather than doing justice to the book. But, pity or not, it is another fact of life.

I myself was for ten years children's book review editor of a newspaper (the *Guardian,* formerly *Manchester Guardian*). During that time I was frequently asked how reviewers were selected, what criteria they were expected to apply, and how I chose the books to be reviewed and allotted the reviews their appropriate length and prominence. It seems worthwhile to try to answer these questions now. They are not quite such separate questions as they may appear, and the answers will overlap.

Let us look at criteria first. Here I think we can distinguish between creative work—fiction, poetry, and picture books—on the one hand and information books on the other. It is possible to lay down basic and fairly consistent criteria for information books: Are they accurate and up-to-date? Are they fair? Are they clear and comprehensible? Do the format and illustrations aid understanding? Do they offer useful suggestions for further reading and, if appropriate, an index? Do they—and this is particularly important with information books for young children—stir the imagination rather than bury it under a pile of facts? And—an easy criterion to state but a very difficult one to apply—are they really *necessary*, or are they just adding one more to a series and repeating what can already be found elsewhere?

For creative work it is much harder to lay down formal criteria, and in my opinion a review editor should not try to do so. A lot of bad reviewing arises from coming to a book with a preconceived idea of what this kind of book should be like, and then praising or slating it according to how far it fits the framework. I think this is a wrong approach. I think that if you are a reviewer you should come to any piece of creative work with as open a mind as possible and ask yourself, "What have we here? What is it trying to do? What has it *got?*" rather than trying to measure it against some theoretical framework.

One problem that arises especially with children's books is the multiplicity of viewpoints from which they *could* be assessed. They could be considered in terms of educational value: Would a particular book, for instance, help a

child with a reading problem or give him some useful historical background? They could be considered in terms of psychological value: Would a book help a child to adjust to his
peer group or family situation? They could be considered in
terms of social value: Would a book help a child achieve the
right attitudes to race, sex, class, or whatever? In a journal
of education, or psychology, or sociology, a reviewer might
legitimately be more concerned with assessment in such
terms than with literary values.

But most newspapers and magazines, and I think most
specialist publications dealing with children's books in their
own right, look at books generally in literary terms rather
than therapeutic ones. And it seems to me that this is right.
Admittedly, reviewers and review editors are open to con-
demnation by professionals in other fields, and still more by
pressure groups, who are convinced that what *they* are concerned with is what really matters, and that the "literary"
person is a mere dilettante. It appears to be widely believed
that literary merit is a kind of ornamentation: the turrets and
twiddles that decorate a building, rather than its essential
structure. I cannot accept this view. To me it seems that a
book is a whole; its style and form are as integral to it as its
content and values, and indeed these various aspects are not
entirely separable. Every self-respecting commentator must
be concerned with them all. A good critic, I believe, will
refuse to take a monocular view, and above all will refuse
to accept that an author's job is to instruct under cover of
fiction. Real books are not written like that.

It is seldom rewarding to assess a book by working
through an analytical routine under such headings as theme,
plot, characterization, and the rest. A good reviewer will be

aware of these and of many other considerations but will not use them as items to be ticked off on a shopping list; she will respond in the ways that the book itself requires. (I am using the feminine pronoun to mean "he or she.") If a reviewer is to concern herself seriously with books for children, she will obviously need a wide knowledge of children's literature; but that is not enough. A person who only knows about children's books is disastrously unqualified for the job. A children's book reviewer should be well informed about literature in general, and ideally about films, theater, and television, too. She should take a lively interest in current affairs and in a wide range of intellectual issues. She should, in fact, have more qualifications than a reviewer of books for adults, because she needs to know all the things you would expect a person interested in contemporary culture and society to know, and she needs to know about children and their books as well. That is a lot to ask of a reviewer, but it has to be asked.

The crucial task of a review editor is to select the right reviewers. My own profound belief, as implied in the previous paragraph, is that the quality and ability of the critic are far more important than the formal criteria, if any, that she employs. Find reviewers whose honesty, perceptiveness, and felicity of expression you can rely on, and trust them totally: that is my recipe for success in editing review pages. It is not the mark of a good editor to edit heavily, or to be constantly appointing and discarding reviewers. A reviewing team should, I think, have a character of its own, and although it should not be unvarying in composition it should have enough continuity to preserve that character.

A question on which there is some disagreement is

whether a reviewer should herself be a creative writer. There may be a distinction to be drawn here between the needs of general and of specialist publications. It is possible that for a specialist publication the reviewer needs to be more fully informed on the availability of other books on similar themes or subjects, and more conversant with the requirements of schools and libraries than most authors are; also that, having an audience that can be assumed to be already interested, the specialist-publication reviewer does not have so much need as in a general publication to produce an attractive piece of writing that will compete successfully with other material for the reader's attention. For a newspaper or general magazine, it seems to me to be desirable that at least some reviewers should be practitioners—provided, of course, that they have critical ability, which not all creative writers have.

An author as reviewer cannot help having a sense of responsibility toward her fellow writers. She knows how much blood, toil, tears, and sweat go into the writing of a book. She knows that it is a fearful responsibility after a couple of hours' rapid reading to pronounce upon what has cost the author months or even years of travail. She knows that adverse reviews hurt, and that although they may be necessary they are not to be indulged in lightly. She knows, or should know, where corners are being cut or where technical obstacles have been surmounted. Just as a writer about, say, yachting will be helped by knowing in her fingers how to handle a boat, so a writer about fiction must be helped by knowing what writing a book is like. Having said which, I must acknowledge immediately that there are many good reviewers who are not practitioners, and some practitioners who are poor reviewers. I would certainly not wish to exclude the nonpractitioner.

One point on which I am not in any doubt is that a reviewer, whether a professional author or not, must be able to write. If her own writing, as displayed in the review, is poor, sloppy, and ill-organized, then I don't trust her judgment. To produce a graceless, nubbly prose is not, in my eyes, a guarantee of superior perception, but rather the opposite.

On the selection of books to be reviewed, I can write only from my own experience. Since the number of books coming in for review during my editorship was large, and the amount of space limited, more than half the children's books received had to be discarded without even going out to a reviewer. This was an agonizing process. A great many books, in fact, were virtually self-rejecting; even so, I always hated to inflict sudden death on such a scale, and tried to avoid throwing out anything that conceivably could be a borderline case. Each reviewer probably received about twice as many books as she could actually discuss, the final choice being left to her. While the overall length of the review would be fixed in advance (subject to negotiation), the allocation of space within the review to different books would be at the reviewer's discretion. If, having one thousand words available, she chose to give six hundred to one outstanding book and divide the rest among half a dozen, that was her privilege.

As a rule, poor books were passed over in charitable silence rather than reviewed adversely. I am aware of the argument that this policy makes children's book pages too bland, but it seems to me that when there is little room in which to talk about good books it is wrong to waste space on bad ones. The main exception is when a highly regarded author writes a bad book. This does need to be pointed out, in fairness to the public and indeed to the author herself.

At present (1981)—in Britain, at least—the reviewing of children's books has been drastically curtailed by adverse economic conditions. In this cold climate, I am particularly worried about the treatment of information books, which are getting far too little attention, and by the increased danger, in dealing with creative writing, that an excellent book by an unknown author, or, still more likely, an excellent book by an author who has previously written rather indifferent ones, slips through the net and doesn't get noticed. One can only hope that a good book will not slip through all the nets—that somebody's vigilance somewhere will retrieve it.

There are books, of course, that will make their way whatever happens. *Watership Down,* for instance, came out at a high price and in an unattractive jacket from a publisher who had hardly been heard of; yet it took off almost at once and its sales soared into the stratosphere. The news about *Watership Down*—first published in Britain as a children's book—got around among reviewers at great speed. But *Watership Down* is exceptional; it has the literary equivalent of that mysterious thing called "star quality" (which is not quite the same as outstanding merit).

In some ways even more reassuring than the reviewers' immediate recognition of *Watership Down* was their recognition a few years ago of *'I Own the Racecourse!'* (American title, *A Racecourse for Andy*) by the Australian author Patricia Wrightson. At that time Mrs. Wrightson was not well known outside her own country, and her earlier books, though good, had not been immensely successful. It was impressive to see how reviewer after reviewer discovered and drew attention to *'I Own the Racecourse!'* I hope that can be taken as a sign that good books do not actually sink without a trace because of the inadvertence of reviewers or review editors. But if ever I wake in the night and worry about reviewing, that is the aspect of it that I worry about.

There is not a great deal of informed comment on the reviewing of children's books; we could do with more. A criticism frequently heard is that reviewers praise books that only a minority of children will read, while ignoring those that most children actually enjoy. This complaint raises issues I tried to deal with in my Arbuthnot lecture in 1971. Briefly it may be said that reviewing seeks to make known the existence of good books, and thereby help them to find their way to as large an audience as possible. Books with nothing but popular appeal to commend them do not deserve or need such a service. Moreover, a poor book, however popular, will always be poor; and poor books are in no way superior to poor films or poor television programs.

It is also suggested frequently that reviewers should state the age and type of child to whom a book will appeal. Actually the majority of reviews do give some guidance, either because of the way the reviews are arranged in the publication or, implicitly, by what they say. But I think it is a mistake to be too explicit. Children are individuals, not types or specimens of an age group. I would prefer a reviewer to address herself sensitively to the book there in front of her, rather than crudely to the assessment of its suitability for some broad notional category of child. The person reading the review knows her own child, or the children in her class or her library, as the reviewer cannot. Fitting the book to the child is something that such a reader can do best for herself; what she needs is information and a reliable opinion about the book.

At present, good reviewers of children's books are probably scarcer than good writers of them. And it is almost as necessary that there should be good and effective writing about children's books as that there should be good children's books. Conceivably, indeed, it is necessary in order that there should continue to *be* good children's books. As the American writer Henry S. Canby, whom I quoted in the foreword to my book of essays, *A Sounding of Storytellers,* points out: "Unless there is somewhere an intelligent critical attitude against which the writer can measure himself . . . one of the chief requirements for good literature is wanting. . . . The author degenerates." Not the least important thing about good reviewing is that it's good for authors, who need to be encouraged, stimulated, disciplined, needled, and challenged into doing their best. And doing their best is the proper task of writers for children as much as any other writers. Only the best will do.

Learning How: Remarks on the Teaching of Children's Literature

∽

Marilyn Kaye

Teaching children's literature has certain built-in rewards. I've never known anyone who truly disliked a children's literature course. No matter how it's taught, the subject matter alone is a sufficient incentive to guarantee enthusiasm. Students enjoy reading the books, talking about them, and rhapsodizing over their favorites. It's always gratifying to find students responding positively to a topic, and it's certainly nice to hear them say how much fun it's been. But the real test comes when we ask ourselves, what are we really teaching them? And what are they learning?

Too often, children's literature courses are reduced to an interminable list of titles and authors and the memorization of minute facts to be tossed back on exams: What book won the Newbery Medal in 1949? Who wrote *A Wrinkle in Time?* In *Charlotte's Web* the pig's name is _____ (fill in the blank).

What we find ourselves needing is a method, an approach to the material. To know who won the Newbery

Medal in 1949 is simply an historical fact; what we want to communicate to our students is why this particular work is deemed exceptional. And while it is important to know the titles of works that have survived the test of time, it is more important to know *why* they have survived. And even that is not enough, for we must prepare our students for the thousands of books yet to come. The *what* and the *who* may provide the background of the course, but it's the *how* and the *why* that deserve more attention. What we're talking about, then, is evaluation.

From the very first, students need to realize that it is their responsibility to develop an expertise in the area of evaluation. For many children, their only contact with children's books will take place in the library and the classroom, and as future librarians and teachers, students must become true authorities on all aspects of children's literature. They are the ones who will pass this literature on to their intended audience. They must emerge from that introductory class with an understanding of the literature—not simply a memorized bibliography of authors and titles, but an actual knowledge of the process through which children's books can be evaluated.

I've often found that students are afraid of literature. Sometimes, those who were exposed to critical theories and explications in their college-level introductory "lit" courses find the scope and process terrifying. The academic terminology, the exposure to intimidating critical texts, the unfortunate misconception that behind each and every simple piece of narrative lies some hidden, deeper meaning—all may contribute to a student's reluctance to explore a work of fiction. These students have no confidence in themselves, and they want precise guidelines through which they can accomplish the task of evaluation. They want some systematic set of rules and regulations that will allow them to make hard-and-fast decisions as to the quality of a work.

As teachers, it is our obligation to allay those fears, but at the same time gently to dispel any notion of precise guidelines and/or checklists. To begin with, each work must be evaluated individually and on its own terms. True, there are general elements that are present in any work of fiction; but true evaluation of a work takes place only when one perceives how these elements operate and combine, and the procedure takes on a variety of formats when one studies an individual work.

I've seen a so-called checklist of criteria by which a work of children's fiction can be evaluated. One of the questions, which was to be answered with a yes or a no, asked, "Are the main characters well developed?" Certainly, this is a central question one must ask of a work; but the notion of being able to provide an automatic response based entirely on instinct strikes me as somewhat irresponsible. For one thing, instinct may rest entirely on the student's personal taste, and students need to realize that, as much as possible, taste must be separated from objective evaluation. Naturally, we respond much more quickly to characters we can identify with, or relate to; we may instinctively appreciate characters who are sympathetic, who appeal to our sense of values, who carry the qualities we admire in people. But this instinct varies from person to person, and embodies the very different "standards" of each individual evaluator.

This is not to imply that students should be discouraged from responding to a character. In essence, this may be the first step in determining how developed that character is. It's perfectly acceptable to make a tentative suggestion that a particular character is well developed because that character seems "real," or because one "knows" that character so well that one could anticipate that character's responses to situations beyond the scope of the novel. But this is just a preliminary step. The essential question is *why*. Why does the character come alive? Why do you feel you know him? *What has the author done to make you believe in him?* Now we're talking about technique, and the time has come to lay instinct aside, begin investigations, and make discoveries.

The discovery process is based on questions built upon responses. We begin with an open question that is tossed out to the entire class; for example, do you see any recurring motifs here? We then entertain suggestions until we hear one that lends itself to perusal. We may then ask, how is this motif developed? With each response, we encourage the student to expand on it through questions designed to help students become more specific, more penetrating. Why is this happening? What does it mean? Is there a motive behind the action? Is it significant? We begin with the obvious, the apparent and reasonably clear-cut elements and their corresponding meanings, and then guide the students deeper into the work. The key words change now. We start using verbs like *suggest, imply, infer.* We have to modify our adjectives and adverbs, prefacing them with tempering agents such as *rather* and *somewhat.* Precision in statement gives way to possibility, and we soften our declarations by qualifying them. We must have some idea of the type of response we are soliciting, while at the same time we must retain a flexibility to allow for the unexpected suggestion. It is a cumulative process, with each question dependent on the response to the previous question, each question carefully posed to lead the students toward some sort of conclusion. It's a painstaking process, but an exciting one. Students begin to see that they are intellectually capable of discovering and identifying elements on their own. And it is at this point that they realize that there are no truths in literary analysis, that nothing is firm, that there are no checklists by which a work can be evaluated because no element in that work can be classified in an absolute or definite way. We can suggest a meaning, we can infer a message, we can see in the work a variety of implications. To reach these suggestions and implications, we encourage discussion and debate.

Frequently, students fear debate. They look to the teacher for answers, and when the teacher initiates a discussion, they may see this as a ploy through which the teacher will isolate those students who know the "right" answer. They need to be reassured that there are no right answers; that the purpose of discussion is to work toward a common goal of understanding. The concept of debate, in this sense, must be presented to them in such a way that they will not perceive it as a battle of wits. We are not pitting one student against the other with the objective of determining a winner. Rather we are attempting to reach a consensus of plausibility as to what a particular work, or some element of that work, *might* indicate, *could* signify.

Naturally, there will be some students who are more perceptive than others. These are the ones who will make the first tentative suggestions, or who will expand on another student's notion and give it more credibility. These are the ones we begin to depend on, the ones who will pull the others along. And there will always be the dull ones, the ones who will simply ride along on the arguments of others, the ones who placidly take their notes and wait for the "consensus" to be reached. At first there may seem to be an inordinate number of the latter. Later, however, as they catch on to the process and gradually lose their fear of committing themselves to a comment, they begin to participate. Their contributions may be limited simply to an additional, minute bit of evidence that corroborates another's suggestion, but what is important is that they become involved in the process. And even if their contributions are negligible, at least they have been exposed to critical thinking.

The process works something like this: The class, having read Paul Zindel's *The Pigman,* is now prepared to discuss it. They have been generally talking about the major themes in the work, and now they need to delve deeper into the various symbols, images, and motifs that develop the theme. The teacher might ask, "Do you see any motifs that seem to appear over and over again?" The students make some suggestions, and one student tentatively points out that John thinks about dying a lot. The teacher picks up on that; she asks if there are other suggestions of death in the novel. One student notes Mr. Pignati's death, another cites the death of Mr. Pignati's wife. There's a moment of silence; no one else seems to have anything more to say, so the teacher throws out a hint: "What about Lorraine's mother?" And someone remembers that Lorraine's mother nurses terminally ill patients; and suddenly another student recalls a brief scene in which a woman wanders through the subway muttering, "Death is coming." A sense of anticipation begins to build, and the teacher keeps up the momentum:

"Where does John go to drink his beer?" and "What happens in Lorraine's nightmares?" Finally, as all reach the discovery of death as a recurring motif, the teacher begins the next series of questions: "How does this motif fit into the themes we discussed earlier?" And the process continues.

Another example: The class has read M. E. Kerr's *If I Love You, Am I Trapped Forever?* and they are discussing Kerr's technique. One student remarks that Kerr manages to portray a realistic romantic relationship between the protagonist and his girlfriend without ever describing the sexual aspects of their relationship. The teacher picks up on this and asks, "How does Kerr accomplish this? Here are two senior high school students who are 'going steady' and we have to assume that they are involved physically as well as emotionally. How does Kerr manage to avoid references to their sexual behavior, and yet at the same time convey a sense of a 'realistic' relationship?" And one student finds a passage early in the work in which the protagonist declares to the reader that he is *not* going to describe the "very personal" aspects of the relationship because he's not writing the book "for a bunch of voyeurs." The students see that Kerr has placed the responsibility for reticence on the protagonist. In this way, she lets the reader know that a physical relationship does exist, but that the reader will not hear any of the details. And at the same time, the students realize that any emphasis on sexual detail could shift attention from the real theme of the work, and make it much less powerful. Through this discussion, they have recognized one single aspect of Kerr's technique that contributes to the overall impact of the story.

Through course assignments, the process of discovery is

extended and adapted on an individual level. An obvious but useful way of reinforcing the process is through the assignment of an analytical paper. Ideally, a student would select one work and analyze it in terms of theme, plot, characterization, etc. However, unless the student is experienced and proficient in the art of explication and interpretation, this may not prove to be the best method. This type of approach to a paper may encourage the student to attempt exactly that which we have been trying to discourage: the tendency to categorize, classify, and force ideas into pigeonholes. Inevitably, certain students will present us with neatly typed papers bound in plastic folders, each page captioned with the "appropriate" heading: THEME, POINT OF VIEW, TONE, etc. The result is simplistic definitions that reflect little if any interpretation.

There are a variety of ways in which we can help them avoid this, and encourage more creative essays. One way would be to help them isolate an aspect of the work that neatly lends itself to examination. The element of characterization, for example, is one that they may find more accessible, or approachable, than, say, style or tone, elements that are more difficult for the novice to analyze. In the novel that embodies memorable characterizations, students can address themselves to explicit questions: Who are the main characters? How are we told about them? How are their personalities revealed? Who are the minor characters? What roles do they play in the development of the story? How do the characters interact? For what purpose? This limitation on the scope of the study will invite students to focus their attention and provide them with a framework that will help them keep the essay under control.

An alternative way to assist them in defining their essays is by allowing them to write a comparative paper in which similar elements in two or more novels are contrasted. For example, students may take two works in which the notion of sibling rivalry plays a major part, and assess the different ways in which two authors develop the same theme.

Another useful assignment involves a comparison of review sources. After reading one specific work, each student locates three or more reviews of that work. The reviews are then compared on various levels: length of review, amount of review devoted to certain elements of the novel, evidence of reviewers' attitude, and so on. For example, does one review concentrate so heavily on plot that other aspects of the novel are neglected? Does a particular review overemphasize possible "controversial" elements that appear in a work? Does the review focus on literary aspects, or potential audience appeal, or both? Is the review specific in its recommendation, or does it simply "present" the work, with actual decision making left up to the reader? Most importantly, has the review left the reader with sufficient information to assist him or her in making a purchase decision? Having read the book itself beforehand, students can then determine what additional information would have been helpful. Students will also get a sense of how different people analyze and assess a work. This lends credence to the notion that there is no one "right" or "proper" evaluation. In assessing the reviews in light of their own reading, students will also get a sense of how one review may appear more "valid" than another through its logical substantiation of critical commentary.

Whatever form the actual course assignments take, the important idea is that they reflect and reinforce the process of evaluation. In a sense, we are not so much teaching a subject as we are teaching a method. The students who emerge from a basic, introductory course on children's literature do not necessarily "know" children's literature, but they should know how to approach it. They have learned an evaluative process that they can apply through all the years and books to come; and as the books pass through their hands, their skills will develop and become more sophisticated.

As teachers, all we can really do is plant the seed, expose them to basic ideas, and hope that the interest that pushed them into children's work in the first place becomes a commitment. With that commitment comes a lifetime of evaluating children's books and placing those books in the right hands. Without a sense of literature, without an understanding of how good literature works, there can be no evaluation; and just as it will be their obligation to choose good books for children, it is our obligation to lead them toward an understanding of what makes the good books good.

REACHING
THE
READERS

Children's Books
and the Librarian

∽

Amy Kellman

"If you write children's novels there is an enormous
army of librarians, teachers, reviewers and booksellers between you and your audience. . . ."[1] In that army to which
Nina Bawden refers are a goodly number of children's librarians doing double duty as reviewers and teachers, whose
impact is felt in several areas of the children's book world.
Some of them even turn into booksellers, which should be
a comfort to the author and artist who can count on them
to use their wide knowledge of the field in stocking their
stores.

Book selection is the professional term for what librarians
consider one of the most important, most satisfying, and
most frustrating parts of their job. The goal is to connect
children and their books by maintaining a book collection
and adding to it. This is a constant challenge that requires
all the professional skills a librarian can muster.

The business of choosing books forces the librarian to
take three distinctive positions: that of consumer, a very

practical role; that of judge, which implies moral and aesthetic decision making; and that of visionary, with the hope that the future will be served by the choices of the present. Not one of these roles is a particularly comfortable one; but all are played each time a librarian chooses books for a collection.

Librarians have a strong practical streak that has been forced to grow out of years of trying to stretch book budgets that consistently shrink. Purchasing the most books for the least money means not only weighing the possible merits of each book, but also wondering if that $7.95 title will fill a collection's needs as well as the book that costs $10.95. A small budget means hesitating to try that special and expensive book that will reach only a limited number of users.

Beyond financial limitations, the process of selection is subject to other factors outside the librarian's control, such as the physical limitations on the size of the collection, and the ever-changing composition of the library's community. These limitations are real, but not necessarily prohibitive. They can act as a challenge for librarians to develop those critical skills that will make for more intelligent selections and more perceptive reader guidance.

The books themselves create their own limitations or problems. Economic, political, and social changes are reflected in what is published for children, as well as for adults. When the world moves as quickly as it did in the 1960s and 1970s librarians are often left gasping for breath.

In 1964 and 1965 Louise Fitzhugh's *Harriet the Spy* and Julia Cunningham's *Dorp Dead* were major topics of conversation whenever children's librarians gathered. The merits of these books were hotly debated. The discussion did not center on the literary merit of these books, which almost everyone conceded. The concern revolved around the morality and manners of Harriet, a young girl who went around with a notebook spying on people; and the nightmarish experience of a boy who has such a great need for structure that he is tied to a psychotic until it is almost too late to free himself.

Marjorie Fiske best summed up the situation when she observed, "The discrepancy between theory and practice in book selection is often attributed to a time lag in the adaptation of professional philosophy to social change."[2] This time lag works on the professional community, which becomes its own worst enemy by indulging in self-censorship, and on the adult lay community, which reacts by pressuring librarians to remove or not purchase materials that reflect a reality they are not ready to handle or to allow their children to handle.

The problem is to recognize that point at which the process of selection ends and censorship begins. Although much has been written on the subject, little has been discovered to help the troubled librarian. One perspective on the problem is that authors who write children's books are not working for librarians, who must deal with different problems and issues, but for themselves. An author's conception of a children's book grows as his or her own work matures. John Rowe Townsend explains, "There may well be a tendency among such writers . . . to stretch the conventional bounds of the children's book quite unconsciously in the normal course of stretching their own imagination."[3]

The controversy over selection versus censorship will

no doubt continue as long as the process of choosing books does. With time and experience, children's librarians do learn to factor in such diverse elements as literary and artistic standards, the usefulness of a book to the community being served, the gap it will fill in the collection, or the depth it will bring to an area of interest, as well as those financial and space limitations that intrude regularly.

The ideal book selector is an objective judge who understands literary values, who knows the informational and recreational needs of the community being served, and who is thrifty, helpful, and wise. This paragon sees the difference between a social problem novel that is serious and one that is merely sensational, can detect inaccuracies in various works of nonfiction, absorbs new trends with aplomb, and has an artistic eye for picture books that is the envy of many a Caldecott Committee member (the Caldecott Committee is a committee of the Association for Library Service to Children of the American Library Association that annually selects "the most distinguished American picture book for children").

In the real world, however, librarians bring their own very subjective selves to the task. Yet they can temper personal prejudices and preferences with the professional demands involved in book selection. Despite all the limitations both within and beyond the control of the children's librarian the selection process continues—and what a rewarding activity it is, given the fresh and original books that are being published each year. This is an incredible time to be in a position to buy books for children. Among the two thousand plus books published for children each year in the United States are a number that are mediocre, poorly done, and, even worse, dull. But also within this number are diversity, creativity, and originality that make one's head spin.

Picture books are illustrated with watercolors, pen and ink, woodcuts, collages, and black-and-white, two-color, three-color, and full-color processes. The styles can be cartoonlike, abstract, realistic, and all the shades within those categories. The spareness of M.B. Goffstein, the versatility of Diane and Leo Dillon, the sumptuousness of Susan Jeffers' work, and the glowing colors of Uri Shulevitz are only a few of the riches found in this format.

The novel ranges from the warmth and humor of Beverly Cleary and the heightened experiences in Lois Lowry's books to the mystical quality in Virginia Hamilton's work. Humor, fantasy, "problem" novels, science fiction, and mysteries are only a sample of the genres available.

Nonfiction runs the gamut of all subjects open to human investigation. Science is clearly explained and explored by Isaac Asimov, Laurence Pringle, Millicent Selsam, and Alvin and Virginia Silverstein. History comes alive through the work of Jean Fritz, Milton Meltzer, and Mary Kay Phelan. Alice Elizabeth Chase, John Langstaff, and Christine Price have brought the arts closer to children.

Not all the books by these creative people (and the myriad not mentioned) are equally accessible or "comfortable." Some books are automatically taken from a shelf by children because the cover is irresistible or because word of mouth has presold them. Other books of equal and sometimes greater value do not sell themselves so easily. These are the ones that are often not purchased because they are dubbed "shelf sitters"—books that are not read but simply take up space on the shelf. To these books the librarian has a dual responsibility. Selecting and adding them to the library's collection is certainly the first step. There is also the responsibility to see that they are shared with children. Books like *How Does It Feel to Be Old* by Norma Farber, *The Little Fishes* by Erik Haugaard, and Susan Cooper's *The Dark Is Rising* need to be introduced. Whatever technique the individual librarian uses, chances are that with some effort and personal interest these books can be kept off the shelf and in the hands of children, where they belong.

As children's librarians we have first access to the work of people like Nina Bawden, Eleanor Cameron, Florence Parry Heide, Maurice Sendak, and Peter Spier. We have the obligation to share all this talent with as many people as we can. The roll call of authors and illustrators for children is lengthy, and each publishing season adds a few more to watch for. It is clear from their books that they are taking pride in their work and their audience. Children's librarians share their pride.

Librarians who work with children have an image problem that surfaces most often in connection with the books they choose for their library. They are called, in turn, prudish, racist, sexist, knee-jerk liberals, and insensitive clods. For the sake of the profession, the children, and the authors and illustrators whose books speak to children, let John Rowe Townsend's impression prevail: "I have said before, and firmly believe, that on balance the children's library has been a blessing to authors and publishers as well as to children and has made possible the writing and publication of many excellent books which otherwise could never have appeared."[4]

1. Nina Bawden, "The Imprisoned Child," *The Thorny Paradise Writers for Children* (London: Kestrel Books, 1975), p. 63.

2. Marjorie Fiske, *Book Selection and Censorship: A Study of School and Public Libraries in California* (Berkeley: University of California Press, 1959), p. 64.

3. John Rowe Townsend, "An Elusive Border," *Crosscurrents of Criticism: Horn Book Essays 1968–1977* (Boston: The Horn Book, 1977), p. 45.

4. *Ibid.,* p. 44.

Notes on the
First Amendment
and Protecting Children

❧

John Donovan

1. THE FIRST AMENDMENT to the United States Constitution:

> Congress shall make no law respecting an establishment of religion, or prohibiting the free exercise thereof; or abridging the freedom of speech, or the press; or the right of the people peaceably to assemble, and to petition the Government for a redress of grievances.

2. ANALYSTS CONCLUDE that the First Amendment has been viewed throughout its history in two markedly different ways. The absolutist view has been that *no* laws, whatsoever, may be made that would inhibit the rights guaranteed by the First Amendment. The opposing view is that the First Amendment merely accepts the tenets of British

common law, expressed by Sir William Gladstone in his *Commentaries on the Laws of England:* ". . . liberty of the press consists in laying no *previous* restraints upon publications, and not in freedom from censure for criminal matter when published. Every freeman has an undoubted right to lay what sentiments he pleases before the public; to forbid this is to destroy the freedom of the press; but if he publishes what is improper, mischievous, and illegal, he must take the consequences of his own temerity. . . ."

The U. S. Supreme Court has never accepted the absolutist position, advocated consistently throughout his service on the Court by Justice Hugo Black, and to only a slightly lesser extent by Justice William O. Douglas; nor has the Court subscribed without reservation to the opposite view. It is useful in examining the First Amendment to recall that the Bill of Rights—the first ten amendments tell people what rights they have reserved, while the body of the Constitution tells us how the government is to be organized and to function—was designed to still the reservations many patriots had toward the Constitution; also to note that the freedoms relating to religion, speech, and assembly are the *first* amendment to the Constitution. On the other hand, some Constitutional specialists suggest that the incorporation of free speech into the First Amendment was accidental, and that as there was no other logical place to fit it in, it became part of the First by default.

3. THE LANGUAGE "Congress shall make no law" has not been interpreted literally. First Amendment cases have got into the courts as a result of rules and regulations made

by any governmental body, or even nongovernmental bodies, such as a college or university. The rules or laws of any official or quasi-official body prohibiting the expression of rights guaranteed by the First are subject to judicial review if challenged.

Rules, regulations, guidelines, etc., by pressure groups —in contemporary times by groups closely associated with social action causes—have no status at law, however influential they might be on creators of books, films, and other materials. Their promotion by pressure groups is, of course, fully protected by the First.

4. FOR PURPOSES OF THESE NOTES, it is not necessary to comment in detail on all the rights that are a part of the First Amendment and have been examined in the courts. Even so, so that the freedoms of speech and of the press will not seem to exist independently of other rights guaranteed in the First, it is appropriate to refer to other First Amendment causes.

Religious issues have come before the courts often. Contemporary contentious issues that have been examined have included financial aid to religious schools, "released time" from public schools for the study of religion, Bible reading and praying in public schools, service in military forces by conscientious objectors, and Sunday closing laws. To oversimplify, court decisions tend to reflect one or the other of two opposite theories. One is that the First Amendment intends that there be an absolute separation between Church and State, while the other is that the government may not show *preferential* treatment to any religion.

The rights to assemble and petition have been before

the courts, particularly at a time when political and student groups have been denied these rights. Factors *surrounding* assemblies, rather than the assemblies themselves, seem to determine whether or not denials of this right are enforceable. Cases such as those involving the Hatch Act, academic freedom, and political organizing on campus have seen the Supreme Court validating a law barring Federal employees from partisan political conduct, while also striking down college regulations that denied students the right to establish a chapter of the Students for Democratic Society at a Connecticut college if the college was attempting to inhibit "the right of individuals to associate to further their political beliefs."

5. BEGINNING IN THE EARLY 1960s with the publication of what came, by the 1970s, to be referred to as "the new realism" genre of children's books, communities in the United States began to express interest in and concern about the tone and language in many contemporary children's books and, especially, in books published for young adults. During the decade and a half that followed, many books found themselves the object of intense scrutiny in communities nationwide. Books in school libraries were especially examined, presumably because most children in a community attend schools, unsupervised by parents, while, theoretically at least, books available for circulation at a public library or for purchase in a bookstore may be examined by a parent or guardian before being read or purchased.

As a result of increasing interest in the books available to children in schools, parents and parent groups began to urge schools to remove books from classrooms and school libraries if the books were thought to be offensive or hurtful to children. So widespread did this activity become that the National Council of Teachers of English developed a procedure and a form designed to help schools deal with parents seriously concerned about reading and other materials they believed inappropriate for their children. The procedures and form were adapted for use by the American Library Association as well. The purpose of the form has been to assist parents in stating their objections to materials in ways that will allow schools to respond to objections, and also to explain to parents the materials selection policies that have resulted in the purchase of a wide variety of books, films, recordings, and other materials that complement the curriculum and may also enrich a young reader in other ways.

It happens that parents often find themselves unsatisfied with a school's response to requests to remove materials, so they carry their objections, first, to school boards, composed most often of local taxpayer citizens elected to these posts. A hearing or series of hearings about a book customarily takes place at this point. As the verbal exchanges on such occasions are more lively than most at school board meetings, local newspapers tend to print detailed accounts of these events. It frequently happens that citizens are dissatisfied with a school board's disposition of such cases, which are then shifted from the administrative jurisdiction into the courts.

6. EVERY COMMUNITY in the United States has local statutes designed to protect minors from a variety of abuses and injuries. Many communities have statutes protecting minors from "harmful matter."

*   *   *

7.   WHILE THE FIRST AMENDMENT deals with religious issues and the rights of petition and assembly, it is associated in the minds of many persons mainly with free speech and freedom of the press, probably because there has been an astonishing body of free speech/free press case law, but also because the press vigorously reports developments in this area, covering, as it does, the press itself.

It is accepted that freedom of speech and of the press includes all of the communication industries, and a very wide variety of expressions.

Speech and communication are protected by the First, although some expressions are not considered speech by the courts, but action, which has no First Amendment protection: somebody exhorting his fellow citizens to ignore the draft is protected under the First Amendment, but if as part of his exhortation he burns his draft card before an assemblage, he may have broken a law and would be subject to prosecution, not for protesting the draft, but for burning his card, which is judged to be an act, not an expression. What if, in error, the protester burned his library card, not his draft card? Unless burning a library card is an act that is against the law, the protester would probably be exempt from prosecution. Except, what if the assemblage *believed* it was a draft card that was being burned?

8.   COURT-IMPOSED LIMITATIONS on free speech exist in spite of First Amendment guarantees. Justice Oliver Wendell Holmes' 1919 Court decision upholding the gov-

ernment's right to restrict the Socialist Party from circulating political documents among members of U. S. Armed Forces contains the famous language, "the most stringent protection of free speech would not protect a man in falsely shouting fire in a theater and causing a panic." Holmes created the "clear and present danger" justification for restricting free speech. The doctrine has been changed in numerous ways since 1919, especially during the post-World War II Communist scare when "evil" forces were seen in our midst by so distinguished a jurist as Judge Learned Hand, whose decision, affirmed by the Supreme Court, denying free speech to American Communists was based on the *probability* that they were dangerous.

The use of "fighting words" that breach the peace is not protected by the First. At a time when the presence of the government may seem pervasive, some government declarations have been construed by the courts to have a "chilling effect" on free speech and have been declared unconstitutional on the theory "that the possible harm to society from allowing unprotected speech to go unpunished is outweighed by the possibility that protected speech will be muted."

The courts balance "the competing private and public interests." Philosophy, politics, and attitude influence the interpretation of our laws; this fact is nowhere more obvious than in First Amendment cases.

9. OBSCENITY is not protected by the First Amendment.
    The best and most accessible exploration of the Su-

preme Court's handling of contemporary obscenity cases is in Gay Talese's 1980 bestseller *Thy Neighbor's Wife.*

People accused of violating obscenity laws assert that their communications are not obscene and are protected under the First Amendment. The Supreme Court has guidelines for determining whether or not communications are obscene. While the guidelines have evolved from the 1957 *Roth* case, they have been modified on numerous occasions, mainly in the 1973 *Miller* v. *California* case, where the guidelines were enumerated:

a. whether the average person applying contemporary community standards would find that the work taken as a whole appeals to prurient interest;

b. whether the work depicts or describes, in a patently offensive manner, sexual conduct specifically defined by the applicable law; and

c. whether the work, taken as a whole, lacks serious literary, artistic or scientific value.

While the guidelines are "liberal" in certain respects (e.g., it is the "average person" in a community whose standards are the measure; obscenity cannot be judged on passages taken out of context; the appeal to prurient interest must be "patently offensive"; etc.), they are also inhibiting, especially in respect to obscenity being measured by community standards. In a country as large as the United States there are thousands of standards of morality.

*   *   *

10. CHILDREN *per se* are not mentioned in the Constitution. Laws designed to protect children exist in great number, particularly state laws prohibiting the employment of minors. Most laws pertaining to children prohibit them from doing something (such as buying drugs, alcohol, weapons) or going somewhere (to theaters, pool halls, bars, for example).

In First Amendment cases, it has been an assumption by courts that rights guaranteed when communications are to adults are not guaranteed if the message reaches children. Passages in court decisions assert over and over that there is a double standard: that what is not obscene for an adult may well be obscene for a child. Justice William Brennan, who has written many decisions in First Amendment obscenity cases, has put it:

> . . . while I cannot say the interest of the State—*apart from the question of juveniles* and unconsenting adults—are trivial or nonexistent, I am compelled to conclude that these interests cannot justify machinery that inevitably results from state efforts to bar the distribution even of unprotected material to consenting adults. . . . I would hold, therefore, that *at least in the absence of distribution to juveniles* or obtrusive exposure to unconsenting adults, the First and Fourteenth Amendments prohibit the state and federal governments from attempting wholly to suppress sexually oriented materials on the basis of their allegedly "obscene" contents. . . . (Emphasis added.)

11. NOBODY has successfully defined obscenity. Supreme Court Justice Potter Stewart has written, "(all I can say is that) I know it when I see it."

Is anything *inherently* obscene?

12. CHARLES REMBAR, a distinguished lawyer involved with numerous important First Amendment cases, including *Lady Chatterley's Lover* and *Fanny Hill,* suggested in a provocative *Atlantic Monthly* article in 1977 that "we abandon the word obscenity. I do not mean that the law should ignore all the many and varied things that legislatures and courts have tried to deal with under this rubric. My suggestion rather is that we drop the word and turn our attention to the social interests actually involved. Then, perhaps, some sensible law-making and law-enforcement will follow."

Rembar suggests that the "social interests actually involved" are associated with the preservation of our privacy and the elimination of nuisances in our lives. It is the brashness of the pornographer that offends the public more than the pornography. Society should protect everybody's privacy as vigorously as possible, and through laws and regulations that preserve everybody's rights—the right of people to patronize films and purchase magazines, and the right of other people *not* to.

13. MANY CHILDREN'S BOOKS, young adult books, and adult books that are widely read by young people have been removed from schools and libraries. The reasons for removal have varied, but the basic reason has been that an

attempt to impose moral standards through anti-obscenity laws has been pressed.

If, as seems possible, there is no such thing as obscenity, or that obscenity is impossible to define, what, in fact, constitutes "harmful matter" for a child—Mickey's penis? thirty hours of television weekly? Who is to judge? Parents? Teachers? Doctors? And by whose standards? Their own? Publishers' and broadcasters'? The child's?

14.   VERY TRICKY STUFF.

Some International Aspects of Children's Books

∽

Mary Ørvig

The United Nations' International Year of the Child (1979) brought with it a good many public statements and well-chosen words intended to heighten public awareness of the needs and situations of children around the world, in hope of promoting their welfare. It was pointed out that special attention should be devoted to the bypassed children of the Third World and also to the children of immigrant workers, who, along with their relations, often lead rootless existences in a new country that is all too often a hostile environment. More attention should be paid to children with physical or mental disabilities. The Year of the Child was meant to stimulate the 152 member countries of the UN to more concrete action on behalf of all children.

The children's year and its related questions—unlike the women's year and the matter of equality between women and men—was not controversial. There are few people who believe that children should not be well cared for. However, it is not equally obvious to all that specific steps must be taken to deal with key children's issues. The prospects for achieving desired results differ markedly in various countries.

Though I would like to assume that everyone is well aware of the aims of the November 20, 1959, UN Declaration of the Rights of the Child, I think it would be useful, in somewhat abbreviated form, to review it here.

Declaration of the Rights of the Child:

1. The child shall enjoy special protection, and shall be given opportunities and facilities, by law and by other means, to enable him to develop physically, mentally, morally, spiritually and socially in a healthy and normal manner and in conditions of freedom and dignity. In the enactment of laws for this purpose, the best interests of the child shall be the paramount consideration.

2. The child shall be entitled from his birth to a name and a nationality.

3. The child shall enjoy the benefits of social security. He shall be entitled to grow and develop in health to this end; special care and protection shall be provided both to him and to his mother, including adequate prenatal and postnatal care. The child shall have the right to adequate nutrition, housing, recreation and medical services.

4. The child who is physically, mentally or socially handicapped shall be given the special treatment, education and care required by his particular condition.

5. The child, for the full and harmonious development of his personality, needs love and understanding. He shall, wherever possible, grow up in the care and under the responsibility of his parents, and, in any case, in an atmosphere of affection and of moral and material security; a child of tender years shall not, save in exceptional circumstances, be separated from his mother. Society and the public authorities shall have the duty to extend particular care to children without a family and to those without adequate means of support. Payment of State and other assistance towards the maintenance of children of large families is desirable.

6. The child is entitled to receive education, which shall be free and compulsory, at least in the elementary stages. He shall be given an education which will promote his general culture and enable him, on a basis of equal opportunity, to develop his abilities, his individual judgement, and his sense of moral and social responsibility, and to become a useful member of society.

7. The best interests of the child shall be the guiding principle of those responsible for his education and guidance; that responsibility lies in the first place with his parents. The child shall have full opportunity for play and recreation, which should be directed to the same purposes as education; society and the public authorities shall endeavour to promote the enjoyment of this right.

8. The child shall in all circumstances be among the first to receive protection and relief.

9. The child shall be protected against all forms of neglect, cruelty and exploitation. He shall not be the subject of traffic, in any form. The child shall not be admitted to employment before an appropriate minimum age; he shall in no case be caused or permitted to engage in any occupation or employment which would prejudice his health or education, or interfere with his physical, mental or moral development.

10. The child shall be protected from practices which may foster racial, religious and any other form of discrimination. He shall be brought up in a spirit of understanding, tolerance, friendship among peoples, peace and universal brotherhood, and in full consciousness that his energy and talents should be devoted to the service of his fellow man.

It is the final, tenth point—which says among other things that the child has a right to be brought up in a spirit of peace and friendship—that we should consider here. But first a few words on the current physical situation for many children.

There are in the world today 1.5 billion children under the age of fifteen—that is, more than one-third of the world's entire population. Three-quarters of these children live in underdeveloped countries. It is estimated that at least 200 million children will never learn to read, write, or do arithmetic. At least 500 million are threatened with acute malnutrition. In addition, severe nutritional deficiency is a constant threat to numerous children in the developing countries. Inga Thorson, at present Sweden's chief delegate to the Geneva disarmament conference, often ends her speeches with the thought that if the world's total military costs were cut by 5 percent (25 billion U.S. dollars) nine large development projects could be carried out in poor countries. Naturally, all nine would affect children, but these particular projects might be involved:

• 200 million undernourished children could get enough food rich in protein to achieve full physical and mental development.

• 100 million children who do not now go to school could be put through school.

During the international children's year those of us who work with or for children in various areas encountered expressions of great benevolence, but unfortunately very little more than that came of it. For this reason I would like to cite a few facts here from the *UNESCO Statistical Yearbook* (1976):

The annual cost of a schoolchild (estimated in U.S. dollars) in the elementary and intermediate grades:

Kenya	34.9 (1972)
U.S.A.	1090.8 (1974)
Colombia	16.3 (1973)
Bangladesh	4.2 (1973)
Sweden	2024.4 (1974)

The number of children's books produced annually in the same countries:

Kenya	15 (1973)
U.S.A.	2292 (1975)

Colombia	16 (1975)
Bangladesh	2 (1974)
Sweden	861 (1975)

I would like to make one further comment on the UN declaration. If the declaration is to have any meaning at all and not amount to mere rhetoric, its mandates should somehow be integrated into domestic legislation. One may have good grounds to wonder how many of the countries that endorsed the document have during the past twenty years undertaken the required overhaul of their laws in order to improve the status of their children.

Charity begins at home. When I posed this question, therefore, I thought I should examine the situation of my own country. Here I have had access to special material produced by Ulla Jacobsson, assistant professor in procedural law at the University of Stockholm. During 1978 she published a book entitled *Ett barns rättigheter*—the title means Children's Rights—and in 1979 she presented comprehensive material on the legal security of children at the inter-Nordic meeting of attorneys in Copenhagen. Although a great deal of reform work is going on in Sweden in a number of legislative areas (also affecting children), Dr. Jacobsson believes that there is not enough attention being paid to the demands made in the UN declaration. All legal texts that affect children—and there are a great many of them—are written from the point of view of the guardians. They are not written for the children themselves. She believes that laws and ordinances should be written in such a way that children themselves are able to understand what affects their position in society.

Together with another well-known Swedish attorney, Sten Losman, Dr. Jacobsson is writing a book with the working title of *Barnens lagbok* (The Children's Law Book). Their intention is to make the text so easy to understand that children in school will be able to read it. She has stirred up a good deal of controversy over, among other things, her suggestion that children should have the right to get a divorce from unfit parents.

It would have been desirable for the International Year of the Child to have offered as many people and occupational groups as possible further information on children's physical, psychological, social, and cultural conditions. Unfortunately, all too often this sort of information is inadequate, even among individuals who work with or for children. There are several reasons for this, but it is mainly a result of the child's inferior human and social status in earlier times as well as today.

Copenhagen's famous sculpture museum, the Glyptotek, featured an interesting exhibition in 1979 entitled "Children During Antiquity." It was a fairly small-scale but lovely exhibition with an informative catalogue reviewing the relevant literature. It is sobering to see how very scanty this literature—and hence our knowledge—actually is. Consider, by way of contrast, the vast amount of literature the world possesses on, for example, old Greek vases.

Indeed, the child has been almost invisible in history, even less visible than the woman. Granted, occasionally a royal or aristocratic child can be observed. But only during the most recent decades has interest finally been kindled in historical considerations of children's conditions during different periods, most often in connection with research in the history of the family or the study of the transition from agrarian to industrial conditions of production. In recent years a number of professional historians have attempted to survey the brutality against children in earlier times and to document their defenselessness and lack of rights. It is the well-to-do and rather well-equipped children the documents generally tell about. The poor and nameless, on the other hand, we know less about.

In an important work from the 1960s, the French historian and demographer Philippe Ariès discussed the concept of childhood and the changes it has undergone through the centuries. During the Middle Ages childhood was not thought of as a separate period in human life. After the first years of early childhood, children became a part of the adult world during working hours as well as in leisure time. Children and adults participated in the same games and diversions. Schooling—among the social classes for whom the question was ever raised—was not strictly segregated by age or connected with the period of childhood and youth.

Not until the seventeenth century did the image of the child become that of a weak and innocent creature in need of upbringing and protection. People began to take an interest in children's special characteristics, psychology, and needs. Their existence was cut off from the adults' life through special games and the activities of child rearing. Schooling became segregated by age and severed from the older people's world. Ariès thinks that during medieval times there was a direct transition from early childhood years to the adult world while the long childhood of later times was characterized by lengthier efforts in upbringing and education. This reflects the reality of the upper class, the nobility, and the bourgeois groups. But, as Ariès points out himself, among the working classes a long childhood was ruled out by child labor throughout the whole of the nineteenth century.

The children of the masses had to work and work hard. After the first few years of childhood, they had to participate in production, and the working hours could be long and the work heavy. Thus, the transition from childhood to adult life was generally brief and abrupt. It is interesting to note that those during the nineteenth century who were eager to emphasize the moral usefulness of labor (including child labor) seldom endowed their own youngsters with these moral benefits.

What characterized the quick childhood that Ariès so graphically described was the children's proximity to different phases of life—birth, illness, old age, and death. The worlds of children and adults were closely integrated, and early participation in labor was more essential to the families than schooling. Now, most children in industrialized countries have been removed from these different phases of life. Sickness, aging, and death are beyond the child's horizon. As a result, we in the Western world have had to create a special literature for children explaining what really happens in life's different phases.

The sociologists of literature tend to say that each society gets the books it deserves. On the whole, literature functions like any other commercial product. It changes with the market. But there is also, of course, a kind of literature that actively affects and changes the course of events. There are a number of different terms to choose from here: literature, nonliterature; good, bad quality . . . lacking in quality. It is also possible to use words such as *safe* and *unsafe*.

The safe literature is that which usually does *not* question, the sort that comes in glossy, alluring packages and, above all, is low-priced. The safe literature is easily accessible, gives a carefree picture of the world, and does not structure human existence or life values for the young reader. The unsafe children's books pose questions about the real world, viewing reality in different ways, from different angles, offering the child the variety of experiences that comprises reality. The great children's book authors show us this reality by means of realistic description, imaginative escape, or narrative allegory. This literature can be difficult and disturbing, may require reflection, and sometimes is difficult to sell. And in percentage terms there are not enough people in the book business around the world who want to gamble on it.

Very seldom has it been observed how little quality literature for children there actually is in the world, estimated in percentage of the overall production. In countries with a high level of skill in producing children's books, at least there are some alternatives available in opposition to the international trash. In countries that still have not developed to this point, one may simply be suffocated in trivia.

Something we ought to realize is that, viewed internationally, approximately 70 percent of all books produced in the world are originated in these four languages: English, French, Russian, and German, though it is hard to tell how much China produces. The figure applies to adult literature, but also holds good for children's literature. The next step is to present the profile of translations in as many countries as possible. Here we lack information from a great number of language areas. It seems to me that gathering these data is an important task for some of the international children's book organizations. I am going to try to give some examples concerning translation profiles.

Clearly, it is the small European countries with a high living standard, high literacy level, and well-developed book production that top the list in terms of translations. In Denmark, Finland, Norway, Sweden, Holland, Switzerland, and Austria, for example, about 50 percent of children's fiction is translated from the language in which it is first published. The U.S. and the United Kingdom are responsible for the lowest percentages of translations in the accessible material: only 3 to 4 percent of the literature in these large countries is comprised of translations from other languages. Small countries are obliged to learn at an early point how dangerous it is to isolate themselves even in terms of culture. If a nation becomes culturally and politically isolated, it may not be long before it is cultivating chauvinism or inflating the past. But cultural isolation is a threat not only to the small nations of the world; the large ones can also be affected by it if they're not careful. In many countries in the West there is a way of viewing most things in terms of the assumptions of one's own culture: this nearly annihilates an international perspective.

When it comes to the distribution of children's literature and other forms of culture for the young, Sweden has progressed somewhat in comparison with some other European countries. But one of the most important reasons for this is that the basic facts on our children's book production, marketing, and distribution have been stated clearly by a public government investigation summed up in the so-called Literature Report. I would like to give here some facts and figures from this Report.

At the turn of the nineteenth century in Sweden about a hundred children's books came out a year, including reprints and new editions. It is well for us to recall that Sweden for a long time was a poor corner of the world and that not until after World War I was there a turning point in economic and social respects. A contemporary children's book critic could personally survey almost everything that was published in the country earlier in this century. This is no longer possible. Around 1950 the number of titles had grown to 400 annually and, beginning in 1969, the number of publications surpassed 600. In 1975, 861 books were published for children and young adults: that is, one-tenth of the entire Swedish book production. Of these titles (which also include new editions of earlier works and nonfiction books produced directly for children), about 50 percent are translations from other languages—mainly from English and after that, German, French, and Danish. In both children's and adult literature, translations have followed a traditional pattern and have been rather static. The children's book market has been quantitatively dominated by "series of books" of the Blyton and Keene type, which bring up the Anglo-American percentage. At present, three-quarters of all children's book translations in Sweden are done from the English and, all told, over 90 percent come from the four languages mentioned above. This is a characteristic picture in the Western countries; in the Eastern European countries the Russian language plays the same role. If translations are to reflect the children's literature of the world in a more representative fashion—

and naturally that is what we all want—the translating process must be extended to more languages and to language areas beyond the West.

If one further examines the overall assortment of Swedish children's book titles, it appears much too large for the small Swedish language area. Sweden has a population of eight million people and a Swedish-speaking language group in Finland of about 300,000. Not even the most ambitious children's book specialist or critic can follow and actively survey all that is published. The large number of publications would suffice for a language of any dimension. We do not feel that we need these 800 volumes per year.

Since World War II Swedish children's literature has presented a profile that is considered independent as well as ambitious, especially when it comes to the story of everyday life. The idyllic and exotic have had to make way for the reality of children and young people in modern society. The authors' new stance has brought important presentations of thematic areas that had long been forbidden or ignored. One can also see that the original connection between stories of everyday life and the old moral tale, purely in terms of the history and characteristics of the genre, has by no means gone out of existence. Realism is often united these days with the delivery of moral messages.

Six out of every ten volumes of literature translated from the Swedish into other languages are books for children or young adults. From 1970 to 1976 we find nearly 1400 translations of books for children and young adults going abroad, or an average of 200 titles per year. During the same period there were translations into a total of 31 different languages.

One consequence of the large number of translations is that the academic interest in Swedish children's and young people's literature is growing beyond the country's borders. An increasingly important function of the Swedish Institute for Children's Books is to produce information on our children's and young people's books in several of the major languages.

At the annual book fair in Frankfurt in 1978 there was a special children's book exhibition, the "World Children's Book Exhibition," featuring samples of children's books from approximately seventy countries. In the catalogue (entitled *Printed for Children*) one finds the actual book lists and the national summaries and also—if one reads carefully—a certain amount of fragmentary information. Unfortunately, however, a general analysis of the production of children's books was not presented. The publication can nevertheless provide certain clues on what sort of children's books are being offered. The preponderance of imports from English, French, Russian, and German constitutes an overwhelming percentage of titles. Portugal, for example, reports that domestic originals represent 10–15 percent, and countries like Venezuela or Chile bring out ten or so titles of their own a year, but have a flourishing imported Disney culture. The fact is that the great powers of children's books are serving not only themselves but a large portion of the rest of the world. This distribution of books in the world reflects global economic conditions. The printed word, just like everything else in the world, is dependent upon economic power. This is why the children's book people's efforts to promote quality often are so ineffectual.

Interesting reports on this Frankfurt children's book

exhibition were published in Europe. The impressions and opinions were varied, often widely divergent. Two critics with different attitudes were Brian Alderson from Britain and Kerstin Stjärne from Sweden. The former expressed his views in a witty article in the *London Times Literary Supplement* (October 25, 1978) called "Why Ten Wrongs Do Not Make a Children's Right." The latter, writing in a Swedish social-democratic daily, pointed out the many inadequacies of the exhibition and its emphasis on the Western world. *Les extrêmes se touchent.*

I have been working with children's books for a long time and have formulated certain concerns that I think are deeply important. Children's books still have low status, all eager assurances to the contrary. Children's books are still not incorporated as a part of any country's literary history, or put into their educational, social, and literary context.

It is a deplorable fact that no comprehensive cross-cultural comparison exists of the Nordic children's book scene, covering children's books from Denmark, Finland, the Faroe Islands, Greenland, Iceland, Norway, Sweden, and the Lapp language areas. It is a deplorable fact that the entire international children's book field is lacking in comparative studies. The few attempts that have been made consist of the usual ramble around two or three of the major language areas with a sprinkling of titles from other countries. This is well to remember when we—or some of us at least—are wont to stress the internationalism of children's literature.

Paul Hazard, the French scholar of comparative literature, stated the problem in what can be considered one of the first international overviews of children's literature, but to date no one has taken up where he left off. The difficulties are obvious; for example, the knowledge of languages. Here a one-person project is doomed to fail. The only possibility, as I see it, is a cooperative project involving the language areas and countries concerned.

What can one do—what should we do? We must work on two fronts: we must demand more official support and expansion for children's culture, but we must also be on guard against the continued isolation of children's culture. The importance of providing the young with a rich language cannot be emphasized enough. The mastery of language must be a basic prerequisite for the shared human activity we all desire for the young generation in their individual and social lives, for the setting of their future personal, social, and political goals. If we view reading in this larger context, it also appears more evident what a key position the literature of children and young people has, and deserves to have. But we must learn much more about the international picture if children's books are to hold this key position. In order to change attitudes one needs a truthful picture. I feel it is not only time but very urgent for some of the international organizations involved with both the physical welfare of children and the culture of children to get at the real facts and figures. After that it might be possible to see some new concrete roads to follow.

Translated from the Swedish by Verne Moberg
Adapted from a lecture first given October 30, 1979,
at the Department of Scandinavian Studies,
University of Washington, Seattle, Washington

Sources and References
With annotations in English for Danish, Norwegian, and
Swedish titles.

Åberg, Jan-Olof. *Sociologiska aspekter på barnlitteraturen. En genomgång*
(Forskningsrapport 1979:1). Karlstad, 1979. 82 p.
A research report from the university branch in Karlstad, Sweden, about sociological aspects of children's literature. In Swedish.

Alderson, Brian. "Why Ten Wrongs Don't Make a Children's
Right," *The Times Literary Supplement,* October 25, 1978.

Ambjörnsson, Ronny. *Familjeporträtt: Essäer om familjen, kvinnan, barnet
och kärleken i historien.* Stockholm, 1978. 188 p.
Essays on family, women, children, and love in history. In
Swedish.

Ariès, Philippe. *Centuries of Childhood: A Social History of Family Life.*
New York, 1970, 447 p.

Barn, litteratur, samhälle. Kritiska analyser av Pil Dahlerup . . . Stockholm,
1974. 176 p.
Critical essays about children, society, and literature. In Swedish.

Barn och kultur. Ed. Per Schultz. Stockholm, 1972. 247 p.
Children and culture. In Swedish.

Barnens miljö i Norden. Ed. Åke Landqvist. Stockholm, 1979. 96 p.
Children's environment in Scandinavia. In Swedish.

Barnens villkor i Norden. Nordiska teaterkommittén. Rapport från seminariet.
Stockholm, 1978.
The conditions of children in Scandinavia. Report from a semi-
nar arranged by the inter-Scandinavian theater committee. In
Swedish.

Barnmarknad. Kritik av barnmedier och -miljöer. Stockholm, 1977.
256 p.

Critical essays about children's media and environment. In Swedish.

Bell, Anthea. "Children's Books in Translation," *Signal: Approaches to Children's Books.* Lockwood, England, 1979/28, pp. 47–53.

En bok om böcker. Litteraturutredningens branchstudier. Stockholm, 1972. 613 p.
A report from a Governmental Commission with an English summary; including a statistical survey of world book production. In Swedish.

Børnelitteratur i Norden. Nordisk Ministerråd. Sekretariatet for nordisk kulturelt samarbejde. Copenhagen, 1979. 36 p.
Children's literature in Scandinavia. A report published by the secretariat for inter-Scandinavian cultural cooperation. In the different Nordic languages.

Børne- og ungdomsbøger. Problemer og analyser. Ed. Sven Møller Kristensen and Preben Ramløv. Copenhagen, 1970. 285 p.
Critical essays and analyses of literature for children and young people. In Danish.

Children's Books in Translation: The Situation and the Problems (Studies published by the Swedish Institute for Children's Books. 9.). Ed. Göte Klingberg, Mary Ørvig, Stuart Amor. Stockholm, 1978. 173 p.
Collection of essays based on lectures held by members of the International Research Society for Children's Literature at their third symposium in Södertälje, Sweden, 1976.

Children's Literature as a Means of Promoting Intercultural Understanding: Report of the International Seminar in Denmark, 29 August through 2 September, 1977. Danish National Commission for UNESCO. Copenhagen, 1977. 76 p.

Die Dritte Welt im Kinderbuch. Ed. Jörg Becker and Rosmarie Rauter. (Theorie und soziale Praxis. 8). Wiesbaden, 1978. 299 p.

Escarpit, Robert. *Sociologie de la littérature.* Paris, 1968. 127 p.

Forskning och framsteg, Stockholm, 1977/5–6, 104 p.
Forskning och framsteg is a journal published by the Swedish Re-

search Council. This issue deals with the history of the family. In Swedish.

Forskning om barn.
Nine catalogues about the research on children at the universities of Sweden in recognition of the International Year of the Child 1979. In Swedish.

Furuland, Lars. "Barnboksspridningen i Sverige," *Ska vi ge barnen skräplitteratur?* Lund, 1975, pp. 7–28.
A critical article about the output of children's books in Sweden and its marketing, published in a volume in which different angles of the mass-market literature for children is being discussed. In Swedish.

Furuland, Lars. "Books in Sweden," *Current Sweden,* Stockholm, 1974/28. 10 p.
Also published in German and French by the Swedish Institute.

Gisle, Jon. *Ankismen. En djupvetenskaplig studie i Kalle Anka och hans värld.* Stockholm, 1976. 143 p.
A study in depth about Donald Duck and his world. In Swedish.

Graves, Peter. "Swedish Children's Books in Britain," *Signal: Approaches to Children's Books,* Lockwood, England, 1975/18, pp. 137–141.

Grunewald, Karl. *Barn utan barndom. Om hur barn hade det förr i världen.* Stockholm, 1979. 26 p.
Children without childhood: on children's conditions in earlier times. In Swedish.

Hazard, Paul. *Books, Children and Men.* Boston, 1947. 176 p.

Holm, Birgitta. "Kampen om fantasiproduktionen. Reflexioner kring fantasins roll i uppfostran och kulturindustri," *Ord & bild.* Stockholm, 1976/3, pp. 132–145.
Reflections on the role of tales of fantasy in education and the cultural industry. In Swedish.

Hurrelmann, Bettina. "Politische Erziehung durch das Kinderbuch?" *Westermanns Pädagogische Beiträge.* Braunschweig, 1976/28, pp. 152–162.

Institut für Jugendbuchforschung der Johann Wolfgang Goethe-Universität Frankfurt/Main. *Kinder- und Jugendbuchproduktion in deutschsprachigen Verlagen: Statistisches Material zu den Jahren 1970 und 1971.* Frankfurt/Main, 1974. 37 p.
Annual statistical surveys from the Institute published since 1964, mostly stencils.

Jacobsson, Ulla. *Ett barns rättigheter.* Stockholm, 1978. 159 p.
Children's rights. In Swedish.

Johansson, Hans Olof. *Bokens väg. En översikt i litteraturutredningens spår.* Stockholm, 1974. 194 p.
How books are published in Sweden. In Swedish.

Klingberg, Göte. *Das deutsche Kinder- und Jugendbuch im schwedischen Raum.* Weinheim, 1973. 140 p.

Klingberg, Göte. *Översättningen av barn- och ungdomsböcker. En metodisk förundersökning.* Göteborg, 1974. 192 p.
Translation of books for children and young people: a preliminary methodological investigation. In Swedish.

Liljeström, Rita. *Samhället och barns utveckling.* (SOU 1975:31) Stockholm, 1975. 122 p.
Society and the development of the child. In Swedish.

Litteratursociologi. Ed. Karl Erik Rosengren and Jan Thavenius. Stockholm, 1970. 249 p.
Essays on the sociology of literature. In Swedish.

Lundqvist, Åke. *Masslitteraturen. Förströelse—förförelse—fara?* Stockholm, 1977. 173 p.
Mass-market literature: entertainment, seduction, danger. In Swedish.

Mählqvist, Stefan. *Böcker för svenska barn 1870–1950. En kvantitativ analys av barn- och ungdomslitteratur i Sverige* (Studies published by the Swedish Institute for Children's Books. 5.). Stockholm, 1977. 205 p.

Books for Swedish children 1870–1950. A quantitative analysis of children's literature in Sweden.

Mählqvist, Stefan. "Export och import av barnböcker i Sverige," *Barnboken, information från Svenska Barnboksinstitutet,* Stockholm, 1978/1, pp. 4–7.
An article on the export and import of children's books in Sweden published in *Barnboken,* the newsletter of the Swedish Institute for Children's Books. In Swedish.

Meek, Margaret, Aidan Warlow, and Griselda Barton. *The Cool Web: The Pattern of Children's Reading.* London, 1977. 427 p.

Munch-Petersen, Erland. *Hvorfor læser vi triviallitteratur?* Copenhagen, 1974. 135 p.
Why do we read mass-market literature? In Danish.

Nowak, Lilian. *Bokläsaren. En översikt över nordisk forskning efter 1945, med annoterad bibliografi.* Stockholm, 1971, 209 p.
A research survey of reading and reading habits in Scandinavia after 1945, with an annotated bibliography. In Swedish.

Ørvig, Mary. "One World in Children's Books?" May Hill Arbuthnot Honor Lecture, *Top of the News.* Chicago, 1972/4, pp. 399–422.

Paulden, Sydney. "The Nordic Children's Market," *Bookseller.* London, February 18, 1978. pp. 1454–1455.

Printed for Children. World Children's Book Exhibition. Compiled by Rosmarie Rauter. München . . . , 1978. 448 p.

Rudeng, Erik. "Barnet, historien och framtiden," *Ord & bild.* Stockholm, 1979/1, pp. 3–40.
An essay published in the journal *Ord & bild* about the past and future of the child. In Swedish.

Seip, Anne-Lise. "Barnets historie—vår fortrengte fortid?" *Forskningsnytt.* Oslo, 1979/4, pp. 2–6.
The forgotten history of the child. In Norwegian.

Stjärne, Kerstin. *Fler passningar. Om barn, våld och framtiden i världen.* Stockholm, 1979. 287 p.

Critical articles about children, violence, and the future of the world. In Swedish.

Stjärne, Kerstin. *Passningar. Till kritiken av barnkulturen.* Lund, 1977. 288 p.
Articles about children's culture. In Swedish.

The Swedish Literary Commission. *Summary of the Main Report.* Stockholm, 1974, pp. 444–498.

Tellgren, Christina. *Utgivningen av barn- och ungdomslitteratur i Sverige 1966–1972.* Uppsala, 1975. 63 p.
The publishing of literature for children and young people in Sweden 1966–1972. With a summary in English.

UNESCO Statistical Yearbook 1976. Paris, 1977. 1074 p.

The United Nations and Human Rights. United Nations: New York, 1978. 166 p.

World Atlas of the Child. Prepared by the World Bank in recognition of the International Year of the Child. Washington, D.C., 1979. 39 p.

About the Contributors

◡◠

Lloyd Alexander was awarded the 1969 Newbery Medal for *The High King,* the final volume of the *Prydain Chronicles,* and the 1971 National Book Award for *The Marvelous Misadventures of Sebastian.*

Susan Cooper received the 1973 Boston Globe-Horn Book Award for *The Dark is Rising,* and the 1976 Newbery Medal for *The Grey King,* the fourth volume in *The Dark is Rising* fantasy sequence.

Robert Cormier's realistic novels for young adults, which include *The Chocolate War* and *After the First Death,* have stimulated unprecedented discussion and commentary.

John Donovan is Executive Director, The Children's Book Council, and the author of several notable children's books.

Paula Fox received the Hans Christian Andersen Medal in 1978, and the 1974 Newbery Medal for *The Slave Dancer.*

Jean Fritz has written books of historical fiction for children as well as biographies of people in America's past, including *Where Do You Think You're Going, Christopher Columbus?*

Virginia Hamilton was awarded the 1975 Newbery Medal, the 1975 National Book Award, and the 1974 Boston Globe-Horn Book Award for *M.C. Higgins the Great.*

Betsy Hearne is Children's Book Review Editor of the American Library Association's *Booklist* and author of *Choosing Books for Children: A Commonsense Guide.*

Mimi Kayden is Associate Publisher and Marketing Director of Children's Books, Elsevier-Dutton Publishing Company, Inc.

Marilyn Kaye, currently on the faculty of the College of Librarianship, University of South Carolina, is a critic and reviewer of children's books.

Amy Kellman is Head, Children's Department, Carnegie Library of Pittsburgh, and 1980–81 President of the Association for Library Service to Children, The American Library Association.

E.L. Konigsburg received the 1968 Newbery Medal for *From the Mixed-Up Files of Mrs. Basil E. Frankweiler.* In the same year *Jennifer, Hecate, Macbeth, William McKinley and Me, Elizabeth* was named a Newbery Honor Book.

Myra Cohn Livingston is a poet, anthologist, and recipient of the 1980 Excellence in Poetry Award from the National Council of Teachers of English.

Arnold Lobel's Frog and Toad Are Friends *was named a 1971 Caldecott Honor Book, and* Frog and Toad Together *was a Newbery Honor Book in 1973.* Fables *won the 1981 Caldecott Medal.*

David Macaulay's Cathedral *was a 1974 Caldecott Honor Book and* Castle *was a Caldecott Honor Book in 1978.*

Milton Meltzer is a historian, biographer, and author of many notable books for young people, including *Langston Hughes* and *Remember the Days,* both contenders for the National Book Award.

Ursula Nordstrom was for many years Publisher of Harper Junior Books, Harper and Row Publishers, and is now a consultant.

Mary Ørvig been Director of the Swedish Institute for Children's Books since its inception in 1966, and presented the May Hill Arbuthnot Lecture in 1972.

Laurence Pringle is the author of over thirty nonfiction books for children, and in 1978 received the National Wildlife Federation's Special Conservation Award.

Millicent Selsam, known especially for her many science books for young children, was a 1980 nominee for the Laura Ingalls Wilder Award and was the recipient of the Thomas Alva Edison Award.

Maurice Sendak, who contributed the jacket art for this volume, has written and illustrated many books for children, including *Where the Wild Things Are,* for which he received the 1964 Caldecott Medal, and *In the Night Kitchen,* a 1971 Caldecott Honor Book.

Sophie Silberberg is a specialist in promoting and marketing children's books and a past president of The Children's Book Council.

John Rowe Townsend, British author and critic of children's literature, received the 1970 Boston Globe-Horn Book Award for *The Intruder.*

Jill Paton Walsh is a British author of books for young people and recipient of the 1975 Boston Globe-Horn Book Award for *Unleaving.*

06